ISBN 978-1-330-70076-1
PIBN 10094174

English
Français
Deutsche
Italiano
Español
Português

www.forgottenbooks.com

Mythology Photography **Fiction**
Fishing Christianity **Art** Cooking
Essays Buddhism Freemasonry
Medicine **Biology** Music **Ancient**
Egypt Evolution Carpentry Physics
Dance Geology **Mathematics** Fitness
Shakespeare **Folklore** Yoga Marketing
Confidence Immortality Biographies
Poetry **Psychology** Witchcraft
Electronics Chemistry History **Law**
Accounting **Philosophy** Anthropology
Alchemy Drama Quantum Mechanics
Atheism Sexual Health **Ancient History**
Entrepreneurship Languages Sport
Paleontology Needlework Islam
Metaphysics Investment Archaeology
Parenting Statistics Criminology
Motivational

BELL'S ENGLISH HISTORY SOURCE BOOKS

General Editors: S. E. WINBOLT, M.A., and KENNETH BELL, M.A.

CANADA

(1535—PRESENT-DAY)

BELL'S ENGLISH HISTORY SOURCE BOOKS.

Volumes now Ready. 1s. *net each.*

1307-1399. War and Misrule (special period for the School Certificate Examination, July and December, 1913). Edited by A. A. LOCKE.

1154-1216. The Angevins and the Charter. Edited by S. M. TOYNE, M.A., Headmaster of St. Peter's School, York, late Assistant Master at Haileybury College.

1485-1547. The Reformation and the Renaissance. Edited by F. W. BEWSHER, Assistant Master at St. Paul's School.

1547-1603. The Age of Elizabeth. Edited by ARUNDELL ESDAILE, M.A.

1603-1660. Puritanism and Liberty. Edited by KENNETH BELL, M.A.

1660-1714. A Constitution in Making. Edited by G. B. PERRETT, M.A.

1714-1760. Walpole and Chatham. Edited by K. A. ESDAILE.

1760-1801. American Independence and the French Revolution. Edited by S. E. WINBOLT, M.A.

1801-1815. England and Napoleon. Edited by S. E. WINBOLT, M.A.

1815-1837. Peace and Reform. Edited by A. C W. Edwards, Assistant Master at Christ's Hospital.

1876-1887. Imperialism and Mr. Gladstone. Edited by R. H Gretton.

1535-Present-day. Canada. Edited by James Munro, M.A., Lecturer in Colonial and Indian History in the University of Edinburgh.

Other volumes, covering the whole range of English History from Roman Britain to 1887, are in active preparation, and will be issued at short intervals.

LONDON : G. BELL AND SONS, LTD.

CANADA

(1535—PRESENT-DAY)

BY

JAMES MUNRO, M.A.

LECTURER IN COLONIAL AND INDIAN HISTORY IN THE
UNIVERSITY OF EDINBURGH

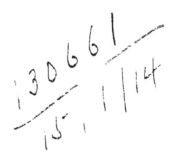

LONDON

G. BELL AND SONS, LTD.

1913

INTRODUCTION

THIS series of English History Source Books is intended for use with any ordinary textbook of English History. Experience has conclusively shown that such apparatus is a valuable —nay, an indispensable—adjunct to the history lesson. It is capable of two main uses : either by way of lively illustration at the close of a lesson, or by way of inference-drawing, before the textbook is read, at the beginning of the lesson. The kind of problems and exercises that may be based on the documents are legion, and are admirably illustrated in a *History of England for Schools*, Part I., by Keatinge and Frazer, pp. 377-381. However, we have no wish to prescribe for the teacher the manner in which he shall exercise his craft, but simply to provide him and his pupils with materials hitherto not readily accessible for school purposes. The very moderate price of the books in this series should bring them within the reach of every secondary school. Source books enable the pupil to take a more active part than hitherto in the history lesson. Here is the apparatus, the raw material : its use we leave to teacher and taught.

Our belief is that the books may profitably be used by all grades of historical students between the standards of fourth-form boys in secondary schools and undergraduates at Universities. What differentiates students at one extreme from those at the other is not so much the kind of subject-matter dealt with, as the amount they can read into or extract from it.

In regard to choice of subject-matter, while trying to satisfy the natural demand for certain " stock ' documents of vital importance, we hope to introduce much fresh and novel matter. It is our intention that the majority of the extracts should be lively in style—that is, personal, or descriptive, or rhetorical, or even strongly partisan—and should not so much profess to give the truth as supply data for infer-ence. We aim at the greatest possible variety, and lay under contribution letters, biographies, ballads and poems, diaries, debates, and newspaper accounts. Economics, London, muni-cipal, and social life generally, and local history, are represented in these pages.

The order of the extracts is strictly chronological, each being numbered, titled, and dated, and its authority given. The text is modernised, where necessary, to the extent of leaving no difficulties in reading.

We shall be most grateful to teachers and students who may send us suggestions for improvement.

S. E. WINBOLT.
KENNETH BELL.

NOTE TO THIS VOLUME

FOR liberty to reproduce the more recent of the extracts here quoted, I have to acknowledge the kindness of Miss E. Pauline Johnson of Vancouver (No. 52) ; of Mr. Charles G. D. Roberts (No. 57); of Mr. F. A. Talbot and Messrs. Seeley, Service & Co., author and publishers of *The Making of a Great Canadian Railway* (No. 55) ; and of Messrs. Constable & Co., the publishers of the late Lord Wolseley's *Story of a Soldier's Life* (No. 48). To several of the sources quoted I was directed by the volume of selections published in 1907 under the title *Canadian Constitutional Development*, by Pro-fessor H. E. Egerton of Oxford and Professor W. L. Grant of Kingston, Ontario, both of whom have also made other helpful suggestions, as has Mr. H. P. Biggar, the representative of the Canadian Archives Office in this country. Finally, the task of finding what one wanted has been very greatly facilitated by the sympathetic aid of Mr. P. E. Lewin, who never loses a chance of making the superb collection over which he presides in the Library of the Royal Colonial Institute useful to anyone who may be interested in the Britains overseas.

J. M.

TABLE OF CONTENTS

CANADA

(1535—Present-day)

1. A GREAT LAND OF RIVERS AND LAKES.

Source.—A Speech delivered by Lord Dufferin at Winnipeg, quoted in *Round the Empire*, by Mr. G. R. Parkin. London, 1893.

As a poor man cannot live in a big house, so a small country cannot support a big river.

Now to an Englishman or a Frenchman the Severn or the Thames, the Seine or the Rhone, would appear considerable streams ; but in the Ottawa, a mere affluent of the St. Lawrence, an affluent, moreover, which reaches the parent stream six hundred miles from its mouth, we have a river nearly five hundred and fifty miles long, and three or four times as big as any of them.

But even after having ascended the St. Lawrence itself to Lake Ontario, and pursued it across Lake Erie, St. Clair, Lake Huron, and Lake Superior to Thunder Bay—a distance of fifteen hundred miles, where are we ? In the estimation of a person who has made the journey, at the end of all things ; but to us, who know better, scarcely at the beginning of the great fluvial systems of the Dominion ; for from that spot, that is to say, from Thunder Bay, we are able at once to ship our astonished traveller on to the Kaministiquia, a river of some hundred miles long. Thence, almost in a straight line, we launch him on to Lake Shebandowan and Rainy Lake and River—a magnificent stream three hundred yards broad and a couple of hundred miles long, down whose tranquil bosom he floats to the Lake of the Woods, where he finds himself on a sheet of water which, though diminutive as compared with the inland seas he has left behind him, will probably be found sufficiently extensive to render him fearfully sea-sick during his passage across it.

For the last eighty miles of his voyage, however, he will be consoled by sailing through a succession of land-locked channels, the beauty of whose scenery, while it resembles certainly excels, the far-famed Thousand Islands of the St Lawrence.

From this lacustrine paradise of sylvan beauty we are able at once to transfer our friend to the Winnipeg, a river whose existence in the very heart and centre of the continent is in itself one of Nature's most delightful miracles—so beautiful and varied are its rocky banks, its tufted islands ; so broad so deep, so fervid is the volume of its waters, the extent of their lake-like expansions, and the tremendous power of their rapids.

At last let us suppose we have landed our traveller at the town of Winnipeg, the half-way house of the continent, the capital of the Prairie Province. . . . Having had so much of water, having now reached the home of the buffalo, like the extenuated Falstaff he naturally " babbles of green fields " and careers in imagination over the green grasses of the prairie Not at all. . . . We take him down to your quay and ask him which he will ascend first—the Red River or the Assiniboine —two streams, the one five hundred miles long, the other four hundred and eighty, which so happily mingle their waters within your city limits. After having given him a preliminary canter up these respective rivers, we take him off to Lake Winnipeg, an inland sea 300 miles long and upwards of 60 broad, during the navigation of which, for many a weary hour he will find himself out of sight of land, and probably a good deal more indisposed than ever he was on the Lake of the Woods, or even the Atlantic.

At the north-west angle of Lake Winnipeg he hits upon the mouth of the Saskatchewan, the gateway of the North-West and the starting-point to another 1500 miles of navigable water flowing nearly due East and West between its alluvial banks.

Having now reached the foot of the Rocky Mountains, our Ancient Mariner—for by this time he will be quite entitled to such an appellation—knowing that water cannot run uphill, feels certain his aquatic experiences are concluded.

He was never more mistaken. We immediately launch him upon the Athabasca and Mackenzie Rivers, and start him on a longer trip than he has yet undertaken—the navigation of the Mackenzie River alone exceeding 2500 miles. If he survives this last experience we wind up his peregrinations by a concluding voyage of 1400 miles down the Fraser River, or, if he prefers it, the Thompson River, to Victoria in Vancouver, whence, having previously provided him with a first class return ticket for that purpose, he will probably prefer getting home *via* the Canadian Pacific.

Now, in this enumeration, those who are acquainted with the country are aware that, for the sake of brevity, I have omitted thousands of miles of other lakes and rivers which water various regions of the North-West: the Qu'Appelle River, the Belly River, Lake Manitoba, Lake Winnipegosis, Shoal Lake, and others, along whose interminable banks and shores I might have dragged, and finally exterminated, our way-worn guest.

2. JACQUES CARTIER'S VISIT TO HOCHELAGA IN OCTOBER (1535).

Source.—Lescarbot's *History of New France,* edited for the Champlain Society, by W. L. Grant and H. P. Biggar. Toronto, 1911.

Early next morning the captain donned his armour and ordered his men to be marshalled in order to visit the town and habitation of this tribe, and a mountain which lies close to the town, whither the captain went with the noblemen and twenty mariners, leaving the rest to guard the boats, and taking three men from the town of Hochelaga to be his guides and escort to the spot. And when on the road we found it as well beaten as could be, in a fair country like a park ; with as fine oaks as in any forest in France, and the whole ground beneath them thick with acorns. When we had gone about a league and a half, we came upon one of the chiefest lords of the town of Hochelaga, with a large company, who made sign to us to rest there beside a fire which they had lighted in the roadway. And then this chief began to make a sermon and discourse, which, as we have already said, is their mode of showing joy and friendship, welcoming the captain and his company ; and our captain gave him two hatchets and two knives, with a cross and a crucifix which he made him kiss, and then hung it around his neck, whereof the chief thanked our captain. This done, we went along, and about half a league further on began to come upon ploughed fields, and fair large meadows full of their manner of corn, which resembles the millet of Brazil, as large as a pea or larger, whereon they live as we do on wheat. And amid these fields is situated and placed the said town of Hochelaga, stretching up to a mountain which lies beside it, which is well cultivated and most fertile, and from whose top one can see to a great distance. This mountain we called Mount Royal. The town is built in a circle, and surrounded with a wooden palisade in three tiers, like a pyramid ; the top row is crosswise, the centre row upright, and the bottom row is laid lengthwise ; the whole compactly joined and lashed together after their manner, rising to about twice the height of a lance. The town has but one gate or entry, closed with bars ; on it and at several points along the wall are galleries of a kind, with ladders ascending to them, provided with rocks and stones for its guard and defence. In the town are about fifty houses, each about fifty paces long or more, and twelve to fifteen broad, built all of wood, with roofs and sides made of strips of bark or of wood as broad as a table, well and cunningly knotted together after their fashion ; within these are several rooms, large and small ; in the midst of each house, on the ground, is a large hall where they light their fire and live in common, afterwards retiring, the men with their women and children, to their said chambers. They also have garners at the top of their houses, where they store their corn, which they call caraconi, whereof they make their bread in the following manner. They have wooden mortars, like those for beating hemp, and in these with wooden beetles they beat the corn to powder, then make paste of it and cakes of the paste, which they put on a hot stone and cover with hot pebbles, and thus they bake their bread, for want of an oven. They also make many stews of this corn, and also of beans and peas, of which they have good store ; also of large cucumbers and other fruits. They have also in their houses large vats like tuns, wherein they store their eels and other fish, which they smoke during the summer and live upon in winter ; of these they gather great plenty, as we by experience have seen. None of their viands have any touch of salt; and they sleep on strips of bark laid on the ground, covered with wretched skins, whereof they also make their garments, such as otters, beavers, martens, foxes, wild cats, roes, stags and other wild beasts, though indeed the greater part of them go practically stark naked.

3. THE FRENCH SETTLEMENT IN THE ISLAND OF ST. CROIX (1604).

Source.—Grant and Biggar's edition of Lescarbot's *History*.

During the above voyage M. de Monts worked away at his fort, which he had placed at the foot of the island, opposite the end on which, as we have said, he had lodged his cannon. This was well thought on, in order to control the whole river both up stream and down. But the trouble was that the said fort faced the north, and was without any shelter, save the trees along the shore of the island, which in the vicinity of the fort he had forbidden to be cut down. And outside the said fort was the barracks for the Swiss, large and spacious, and other small buildings like a suburb. Some had built log-huts on the mainland near the stream. But inside the fort was the dwelling of the said M. de Monts, built of fair sawn timber, with the banner of France overhead. Elsewhere within the fort was the magazine, wherein lay the safety and the life of each, built likewise of fair timber, and covered with shingles. And opposite the magazine were the lodgings and dwellings of MM. d'Orville, Champlain, Champdoré, and other notable persons. Opposite the quarters of the said M. de Monts was a covered gallery, to be used either for sports or by the workmen in wet weather. And the whole space between the said fort and the battery was taken up with gardens, at which every man worked lightheartedly. Thus passed the whole autumn ; and it was not bad progress to have built their houses and cleared the island before winter ; while in these parts pamphlets were being circulated under the name of Master William, stuffed with all sorts of news, wherein among other things this prognosticator said that M. de Monts was pulling out thorns in Canada. And when all is well considered, it may truly be called pulling out thorns to take in hand such enterprises, full of toils and of continual danger, care, vexation and discomfort. But virtue and the courage which overcomes all such obstacles make these thorns to be but gilly-flowers and roses to those who set themselves to these heroic deeds in order to win glory in the memory of men, closing their eyes to the pleasures of those weaklings who are good for nothing but to stay at home.

Having done the things of greatest urgency, and grey-bearded father Winter being come, they needs must keep indoors, and live every man under his own roof-tree. During this time our friends had three special discomforts in this island, to wit, want of wood (for that on the said island had been used for the buildings), want of fresh water, and the night watch for fear of a surprise from the Indians who were encamped at the foot of the said island, or from some other enemy ; for such is the evil disposition and fury of many Christians, that one must be more on one's guard against them than against the infidel. This it grieveth me to say ; would indeed that I were a liar herein, and that I had no cause to speak it. Thus when water or wood was required they were constrained to cross the river, which on either side is more than three times as broad as the Seine at Paris. This was both painful and tedious ; so that very often one had to bespeak the boat a day in advance before being able to get the use of it. On top of this came cold and snow and frost so hard that the cider froze in the casks, and each man was given his portion by weight. As for wine, it was only given out on certain days of the week. Some lazy fellows drank melted snow without troubling to cross the river. In short, unknown diseases broke out, like those which Captain Jacques Cartier has already described for us, of which for fear of vain repetition I shall therefore not give an account. No remedy could be found.

4. THE ANCIENT MARINER (1631).

Source.—*The Strange and Dangerous Voyage of Captain Thomas James to Hudson Bay*, 1631-2 : which is believed to be the source of much of Coleridge's *Ancient Mariner*. Reprinted by the Hakluyt Society, 1894.

[Nov.] I lay ashore till the 17, all which time our miseries did increase. It did snow and freeze most extremely. At which time, we looking from the shore towards the ship, she did look like a piece of ice in the fashion of a ship, or a ship resembling a piece of ice. The snow was all frozen about her. . . .

The three-and-twentieth, the ice did increase extraordinarily, and the snow lay on the water in flakes as it did fall ; much ice withal drove by us, yet nothing hard all this while. In the evening, after the watch was set, a great piece came athwart our hawse, and four more followed after him, the least of them a quarter of a mile broad ; which, in the dark, did very much astonish us, thinking it would have carried us out of the harbour upon the shoals Easter Point, which was full of rocks. It was newly congealed, a matter of two inches thick, and we broke thorough it, the cable and anchor enduring an incredible stress, sometimes stopping the whole ice. . . .

[May.]   The second, it did snow and blow, and was so cold that we were fain to keep house all day.   This unexpected cold at this time of the year did so vex our sick men that they grew worse and worse.   We cannot now take them out of their beds but they would swound, and we had much ado to fetch life in them.

The third, those that were able went aboard betimes to heave out the ice.   The snow was now melted in many places upon the land, and stood in plashes.   And now there came some cranes and geese to it.

The fourth, while the rest wrought aboard, I and the surgeon went with a couple of pieces to see if we could kill any of these fowl for our sick men ;   but never did I see such wild-fowl : they would not endure to see anything move.   . ..

[July.]   . . .   We were continually till the 22 so pestered and tormented with ice that it would seem incredible to relate it.   Sometimes we were so blinded with fog that we could not see about us ;   and, being now become wilful in our endeavours, we should so strike against the ice that the forepart of the ship would crack again, and make our cook and others to run up all amazed and think the ship had been beaten all to pieces. Indeed we did hourly strike such unavoidable blows that we did leave the hatches open ;   and, 20 times in a day, the men would run down into the hold to see if she were bulged.

Sometimes, when we had made her fast in the night to a great piece of ice, we should have such violent storms that our fastening would break, and then the storm would beat us from piece to piece most fearfully ;   other-while, we should be fast enclosed amongst great ice as high as our poop.

5.   TWO ENGLISH EXPLORERS MEET IN HUDSON BAY (1631).

Source.—*The North-West Fox*, Captain Luke Fox's account of his voyage.   Reprinted by the Hakluyt Society, 1894.

[30 Aug.]   I was well entertained and feasted by Captain James with variety of such cheer as his sea provisions could afford, with some partridges; we dined betwixt decks, for the great cabin was not big enough to receive ourselves and followers; during which time the ship . . . threw in so much water as we could not have wanted sauce if we had had roast mutton.

Whereat I began to ponder whether it were better for his company to be impounded amongst ice, where they might be kept from putrefaction by the piercing air ; or in open sea, to be kept sweet by being thus daily pickled. However, they were to be pitied, the ship taking her liquor as kindly as ourselves, for her nose was no sooner out of the pitcher but her neb, like the duck's, was in it again. The gentleman could discourse of Art (as observations, calculations and the like), and shewed me many instruments, so that I did perceive him to be a practitioner in the mathematics ; but, when I found that he was no seaman, I did blame those very much who had counselled him to make choice of that ship for a voyage of such importance. . . .

And (being demanded) I did not think much for his keeping out his flag ; for my ambition was [not so] ethereal, and my thoughts not so airy, so to set my sight towards the sky, but when I either called to God or made celestial observation. To this was replied that he was going to the Emperor of Japan with letters from his Majesty ; and that, if it were a ship of his Majesty's of 40 pieces of ordnance, he could not strike his flag. " Keep it up then," quoth I, " but you are out of the way to Japan, for this is not it." He would have persuaded me to take harbour to winter in, telling me that Sir Thomas Button took harbour the 14 of this instant. Quoth I, " He is no precedent for me. I must parallel my poverty with poor Hudson's, who took no harbour before the first of November ; and that then I durst not take harbour until the midst of the same ; besides, I was not come to do so much as another man, but more than any, as I had already done. . . ."

We parted not until the next morning's dawning, and this 17 hours was the worst spent of any time of my discovery. My men told me his men gave them some tobacco, a thing good for nothing.

6. THE BIRTHDAY OF MONTREAL (1642).

Source.—*The Jesuits in North America*, by Francis Parkman, 1867—
not itself an original contemporary source, but based mainly on a
MS. *Histoire de Montreal*, by Dollier de Casson.

In many of its aspects, this enterprise of Montreal belonged
to the time of the first Crusades. . . .

On the seventeenth of May, 1642, Maisonneuve's little
flotilla—a pinnace, a flat-bottomed craft moved by sails, and
two row-boats—approached Montreal; and all on board
raised in unison a hymn of praise. Montmagny was with
them, to deliver the island, in behalf of the Company of the
Hundred Associates, to Maisonneuve, representative of the
Associates of Montreal. And here, too, was Father Vimont,
Superior of the missions; for the Jesuits had been prudently
invited to accept the spiritual charge of the young colony.
On the following day, they glided along the green and solitary
shores now thronged with the life of a busy city, and landed
on the spot which Champlain, thirty-one years before, had
chosen as the fit site of a settlement. It was a tongue or
triangle of land, formed by the junction of a rivulet with the
St. Lawrence, and known afterwards as Point Callière. The
rivulet was bordered by a meadow, and beyond rose the forest
with its vanguard of scattered trees. Early spring flowers
were blooming in the young grass, and birds of varied plumage
flitted among the boughs.

Maisonneuve sprang ashore, and fell on his knees. His
followers imitated his example; and all joined their voices in
enthusiastic songs of thanksgiving. Tents, baggage, arms and
stores were landed. An altar was raised on a pleasant spot
near at hand; and Mademoiselle Mance, with Madame de la
Peltrie, aided by her servant, Charlotte Barré, decorated it
with a taste which was the admiration of the beholders. Now
all the company gathered before the shrine. Here stood
Vimont, in the rich vestments of his office. Here were the two
ladies, with their servant; Montmagny, no very willing
spectator; and Maisonneuve, a war-like figure, erect and tall,

his men clustering around him—soldiers, sailors, artisans, and labourers—all alike soldiers at need. They kneeled in reverent silence as the Host was raised aloft ; and when the rite was over, the priest turned and addressed them :

" You are a grain of mustard-seed, that shall rise and grow till its branches overshadow the earth. You are few, but your work is the work of God. His smile is on you, and your children shall fill the land."

The afternoon waned ; the sun sank behind the western forest, and twilight came on. Fire-flies were twinkling over the darkened meadow. They caught them, tied them with threads into shining festoons, and hung them before the altar, where the Host remained exposed. Then they pitched their tents, lighted their bivouac fires, stationed their guards, and lay down to rest. Such was the birth-night of Montreal.

7. GOVERNOR FRONTENAC LEADS THE WAR-DANCE (1690).

Source.—F. Parkman's *Count Frontenac and New France under Louis XIV.* (1877). The foot-note appended gives the words of the original French authorities.

Having painted, greased and befeathered themselves, the Indians mustered for the grand council which always preceded the opening of the market. The Ottawa orator spoke of nothing but trade, and, with a regretful memory of the cheapness of English goods, begged that the French would sell them at the same rate. The Huron touched upon politics and war, declaring that he and his people had come to visit their old father and listen to his voice, being well assured that he would never abandon them, as others had done, nor fool away his time, like Denonville, in shameful negotiations for peace ; and he exhorted Frontenac to fight, not the English only, but the Iroquois also, till they were brought-to reason. "If this is not done," he said, "my father and I shall both perish ; but, come what may, we will perish together." "I answered," writes Frontenac, "that I would fight the Iroquois till they came to beg for peace, and that I would grant them no peace that did not include all my children, both white and red, for I was the father of both alike."

Now ensued a curious scene. Frontenac took a hatchet, brandished it in the air and sang the war-song. The principal Frenchmen present followed his example. The Christian Iroquois of the two neighbouring missions rose and joined them, and so also did the Hurons and the Algonquins of Lake Nipissing, stamping and screeching like a troop of madmen; while the Governor led the dance, whooping like the rest. His predecessor would have perished rather than play such a part in such company; but the punctilious old courtier was himself half Indian at heart, as much at home in a wigwam as in the halls of princes. Another man would have lost respect in Indian eyes by such a performance. In Frontenac, it roused his audience to enthusiasm. They snatched the proffered hatchet and promised war to the death.

Then came a solemn war-feast. Two oxen and six large dogs had been chopped to pieces for the occasion, and boiled with a quantity of prunes. Two barrels of wine with abundant tobacco were also served out to the guests, who devoured the meal in a species of frenzy.

[" Je leur mis moy-mesme la hache à la main en chantant la chanson de guerre pour m'accomoder à leurs façons de faire." *Frontenac au Ministre*, 9 et 12 Nov. 1690.

" Monsieur de Frontenac commença la chanson de guerre, la hache à la main; les principaux chefs des François se joignant à luy avec de pareilles armes la chantèrent ensemble. Les Iroquois du Saut et de la Montagne, les Hurons et les Nipisiriniens donnèrent encore le branle: l'on eut dit, Monsieur, que ces acteurs étoient des possedez par les gestes et les contorsions qu'ils faisoient. Les *Sassakouez*, ou les cris et les hurlemens que Mr. de Frontenac étoit obligé de faire pour se conformer à leur manière, augmentoit encore la fureur bachique." *La Potherie*, iii. 97.]

8. MADELAINE DE VERCHÈRES (1696).

Source.—Narrative of the Heroic Deeds of Mlle. Marie-Madelaine de Verchères, aged fourteen years, against the Iroquois, on the 22nd October, in the year 1696, at eight o'clock in the morning,[1] quoted in Mr. E. Richard's *Supplement to the Report on Canadian Archives,* 1899.

I was five arpents away from the fort of Verchères, belonging to Sieur de Verchères, my father, who was then at Kebek by order of M. le Chevalier de Callières, Governor of Montreal, my mother being also in Montreal. I heard several shots without knowing at whom they were fired. I soon saw that the Iroquois were firing at our settlers, who lived about a league and a half from the fort. One of our servants called out to me :

" Fly, mademoiselle, fly ! the Iroquois are upon us ! "

I turned instantly and saw some forty-five Iroquois running towards me, and already within pistol shot. Determined rather to die than fall into their hands, I sought safety in flight. I ran towards the fort, commending myself to the Blessed Virgin. . . .

Meantime my pursuers, seeing that they were too far off to take me alive before I could enter the fort, and knowing they were near enough to shoot me, stood still in order to discharge their guns at me. I was under fire for quite a time, at any rate I found the time quite long enough ! Forty-five bullets whistling past my ears made the time seem long and the distance from the fort interminable, though I was so near. When within hearing of the fort, I cried out: "To arms! to arms ! "

I hoped that some one would come out to help me, but it was a vain hope. There were but two soldiers in the fort, and these were so overcome by fear that they had sought safety by concealing themselves in the redoubt. Having reached the gates at last, I found there two women lamenting for the loss of their husbands, who had just been killed. I made them

[1] Written by Mlle. de Verchères at the request of Governor de Beauharnois.

enter the fort, and closed the gates myself. I then began to consider how I might save myself and the little party with me, from the hands of the savages. I examined the fort, and found that several of the stakes had fallen, leaving gaps through which it would be easy for the enemy to enter. I gave orders to have the stakes replaced, and heedless of my sex and tender age, I hesitated not to seize one end of the heavy stake and urge my companions to give a hand in raising it. I found by experience that, when God gives us strength, nothing is impossible.

The breaches having been repaired, I betook myself to the redoubt, which served as a guard-house and armoury. I there found two soldiers, one of them lying down and the other holding a burning fuse. I said to the latter :

" What are you going to do with that fuse ? "

" I want to set fire to the powder," said he, " and blow up the fort."

" You are a miserable wretch," I said, adding, " Begone, I command you ! "

I spoke so firmly that he obeyed forthwith. Thereupon putting aside my hood and donning a soldier's casque, I seized a musket and said to my little brothers :

" Let us fight to the death for our country and for our holy religion. Remember what our father has so often told you, that gentlemen are born but to shed their blood for the service of God and the king ! "

Stirred up by my words, my brothers and the two soldiers kept up a steady fire on the foe. I caused the cannon to be fired, not only to strike terror into the Iroquois and show them that we were well able to defend ourselves, since we had a cannon, but also to warn our own soldiers, who were away hunting, to take refuge in some other fort.

But alas ! what sufferings have to be endured in these awful extremities of distress ! Despite the thunder of our guns, I heard unceasingly the cries and lamentations of some unfortunates who had just lost a husband, a brother, a child or a parent. I deemed it prudent, while the firing was still kept up, to represent to the grief-stricken women that their shrieks exposed us to danger, for they could not fail to be heard by the enemy, notwithstanding the noise of the guns and the cannon. I ordered them to be silent and thus avoid giving the impression that we were helpless and hopeless.

While I was speaking thus, I caught sight of a canoe on the river, opposite the fort. It was Sieur Pierre Fontaine with his family, who were about to land at the spot where I had just barely escaped from the Iroquois, the latter being still visible on every hand. The family must fall into the hands of the savages if not promptly succoured.

I asked the two soldiers to go to the landing-place, only five arpents away, and protect the family. But seeing by their silence, that they had but little heart for the work, I ordered our servant, Laviolette, to stand sentry at the gate of the fort and keep it open, while I would myself go to the bank of the river, carrying a musket in my hand and wearing my soldier's casque. I left orders on setting out, that if I was killed, they were to shut the gates and continue to defend the fort sturdily. I set out with the heaven-sent thought that the enemy, who were looking on, would imagine that it was a ruse on my part to induce them to approach the fort, in order that our people might make a sortie upon them.

This was precisely what happened, and thus was I enabled to save poor Pierre Fontaine, with his wife and children. When all were landed, I made them march before me as far as the fort, within sight of the enemy. By putting a bold face upon it, I made the Iroquois think there was more danger for them than for us.

They did not know that the whole garrison, and only inhabitants of the fort of Verchères, were my two brothers aged 12 years, our servant, two soldiers, an old man of eighty, and some women and children.

Strengthened by the new recruits from Pierre Fontaine's canoe, I gave orders to continue firing at the enemy. Meantime the sun went down, and a fierce north-easter accompanied by snow and hail ushered in a night of awful severity. The enemy kept us closely invested, and instead of being deterred by the dreadful weather, led me to judge by their movements that they purposed assaulting the fort under cover of the darkness.

I gathered all my troops—six persons—together, and spoke to them thus : " God has saved us to-day from the hands of our enemies, but we must be careful not to be caught in their snares to-night. For my part, I want to show you that I am not afraid. I undertake the fort for my share, with an old man of eighty, and a soldier who has never fired a gun. And you; Pierre Fontaine, with La Bonté and Galhet (our two soldiers), will go to the redoubt, with the women and children, as it is the strongest place. If I am taken, never surrender, even though I should be burnt and cut to pieces before your eyes. You have nothing to fear in the redoubt, if you only make some show of fighting."

Thereupon I posted my two young brothers on two of the bastions, the *youth* of 80 on a third bastion, and myself took charge of the fourth. Each one acted his part to the life. Despite the whistling of the north-east wind, which is a fearful wind in Canada at this season, and in spite of the snow and hail, the cry of "All's well" was heard at close intervals, echoing and re-echoing from the fort to the redoubt and from the redoubt to the fort.

One would have fancied, to hear us, that the fort was crowded with warriors. And in truth the Iroquois, with all their astuteness and skill in warfare, were completely deceived, as they afterwards avowed to M. de Callières. They told him they had held a council with a view to assaulting the fort during the night, but that the increasing vigilance of the guard had prevented them from accomplishing their design, especially in view of their losses of the previous day (under the fire maintained by myself and my two brothers). . . .

On the eighth day (for we were eight days in continual alarms, under the eyes of our enemies and exposed to their fury and savage attacks), on the eighth day, I say, M. de la Monnerie, a lieutenant detached from the force under M. de

Callières, reached the fort during the night with forty men. . . .
So soon as I saw the officer in command I saluted him,
saying :

" Sir, you are welcome, I surrender my arms to you."

" Mademoiselle," he answered, with a courtly air, " they
are in good hands."

" Better than you think," I replied.

He inspected the fort and found it in a most satisfactory
condition, with a sentry on each bastion. I said to him :

" Sir, kindly relieve my sentries, so that they may take a
little rest, for we have not left our posts for the last eight days."

9. THE FRENCH CANADIANS (1737).

Source.—A Memoir transmitted to the French Ministry, probably by
Gilles Hocquart, intendant of New France: quoted in *Documents
relating to the Seigniorial Tenure in Canada*, edited by W. B.
Munro. Toronto, 1908.

La colonie de la Nouvelle-France peut comprendre environ
40,000 personnes de tout âge et de tout sexe, sur lesquelles il
se trouve dix mille hommes en estat de porter les armes. Les
Canadiens sont naturellement grands, bien faits, d'un tem-
pérament vigoureux. Comme les arts n'y sont point gênés
par des maîtrises, et que dans les commencements de l'éta-
blissement de la colonie les ouvriers étoient rares, la nécessité
les a rendus industrieux de génération en génération. Les
habitans des campagnes manient tous adroitement la hache.
Ils font eux-mêmes la pluspart des outils et ustensiles de
labourage, bâtissent leurs maisons, leurs granges. Plusieurs
sont tisserans, font de grosses toiles et des étoffes qu'ils
appellent droguet, dont ils se servent pour se vêtir eux et
leur famille.

Ils aiment les distinctions et les caresses, se piquant de
bravoure, sont extrêmement sensibles aux mépris et aux
moindres punitions : ils sont intéressés, vindicatifs, sont sujets
à l'ivrognerie, font un grand usage de l'eau-de-vie, [et] passent
pour n'être pas véridiques.

C.   B

Ce portrait convient au grand nombre particulièrement aux
gens de la campagne. Ceux des villes sont moins vicieux.
Tous sont attachés à la religion. On voit peu de scélérats.
Ils sont volages, ont trop bonne opinion d'euxmêmes, ce qui
les empêche de réussir comme ils pourroient le faire dans les
arts, l'agriculture et le commerce. Joignons à cela l'oisiveté
à laquelle la longueur et la rigueur de l'hiver donne occasion.
Ils aiment la chasse, la navigation, les voyages et n'ont point
l'air grossier et rustique de nos paysans de France. Ils sont
communément assez souples lorsqu'on les pique d'honneur et
qu'on les gouverne avec justice, mais ils sont naturellement
indociles. Il est nécessaire de fortifier de plus en plus l'exacte
subordination qui doit estre dans tous les ordres, particulièrement dans les gens de la campagne. Cette partie du service
a esté de tout temps la plus importante et la plus difficile à
remplir. Un des moyens pour y parvenir est de choisir pour
officiers dans les costes les habitans les plus sages et les plus
capables de commander, et d'apporter de la part du gouverne-
ment toute l'attention convenable pour les maintenir dans
leur autorité. On ose dire que le manque de fermeté dans les
gouvernemens passés a beaucoup nui à la subordination.
Depuis plusieurs années les crimes ont esté punis, les désordres
ont été reprimés par des châtiments proportionés. La police
par rapport aux chemins publics, aux cabarets, etc., a esté
mieux observée et en général les habitants ont esté plus con-
tenus qu'ils ne l'estoient autrefois. Il y a quelques familles
nobles en Canada, mais elles sont si nombreuses qu'il y a
beaucoup de gentilshommes.

10. THE SUPPOSED WHITE MEN OF THE PRAIRIES (1738).

Source.—The Journal of the French explorer, the Sieur de La Vérendrye, describing an expedition to the Missouri in 1738-9. Printed
in the *Report on Canadian Archives*, 1889.

On the 20th, the whole village set out on the march to go the
seventeen leagues where the meeting-place for the Mandans

had been chosen ; every day they entertained us with the tale that the whites we were going to see were Frenchmen like ourselves, who said they were our descendants. All they told us gave us good hope of making a discovery which would deserve attention. Mr. de la Marque and I made plans along the road from what they were telling us, believing that to be true, from which we had to deduct much. I observed to Mr. de la Marque the good order in which the Assiniboines march to prevent surprise, marching always on the prairies, the hill-sides and valleys from the first mountain, which did not make them fatigued by mounting and descending often in their march during the day. There are magnificent plains of three or four leagues. The march of the Assiniboines, especially when they are numerous, is in three columns, having skirmishers in front, with a good rear guard ; the old and lame march in the middle, forming the central column. I kept all the French together as much as possible. If the skirmishers discover herds of cattle on the road, as often happens, they raise a cry which is soon returned by the rear guard, and all the most active men in the columns join the vanguard to hem in the cattle, of which they secure a number, and each takes what flesh he wants. Since that stops the march, the vanguard marks out the encampment which is not to be passed ; the women and dogs carry all the baggage, the men are burdened only with their arms ; they make the dogs even carry wood to make the fires, being often obliged to encamp in the open prairie, from which the clumps of wood may be at a great distance. On the morning of the 28th, we arrived at the place selected for the meeting with the Mandans, who arrived towards evening—a chief with thirty men and the four Assiniboines. The chief having from the top of a height considered the extent of our village, which appeared of a good size, I had him brought to the hut where I was, where a place had been prepared to receive him on one side of it. He came and placed himself near me ; one of his people then, on his part, presented me with a gift of Indian corn in the ear, and of their tobacco in rolls, which is not good, as they do not know how to cure it like us. It is very like ours, with this difference, that it is not cultivated and is cut green, everything being turned to account, the stalks and the leaves together. I gave him some of mine, which he thought very good. I acknowledged that I was surprised, expecting to see different people from the other Indians, especially after the account given me. There is no difference from the Assiniboines. . . .

I marched in good order to the fort, into which I entered on the 3rd of December at four in the afternoon, escorted by all the French and Assiniboines. We were led into the hut of the head chief. It was certainly large, but not enough to hold all who wished to enter. The crowd was so great that they crushed one another, Assiniboines and Mandans. There was only the place where we were, Mr. de la Marque, his brother and my children, free of them. I asked that the crowd should retire, to leave our Frenchmen clear, and to put their baggage in a place of safety, telling them they had all time to see us. Everyone was put out, but I had been too late. The bag of goods had been stolen, in which were all my presents, through the fault of one of the hired men, in whose care I had placed it before reaching the fort. He had unloaded on entering the hut without looking out for the bag, which he had put beside him in the great crowd. I felt rather confounded, my box lost, my bag of presents, which was very necessary for the place, and there were upwards of 300 livres inside. The Assiniboines seemed greatly annoyed and at once made a strict but useless search. Their fort is full of caves, well suited for concealment. The chief of the Mandans appeared to be greatly moved at my loss, and said for my consolation that there were many rascals among them. He would do his utmost to discover something about it. Had I accepted the offer of the Assiniboines I might have had it found in a little time by force, but I preferred to lose it and to make peace about everything, as I wanted to spend a part of the winter with them to get a knowledge of the more distant country. . . .

. . . The Assiniboines did not yet speak of leaving, although they had purchased all they were able to do, such as painted ox-robes, deerskin, dressed buck skin, and ornamented furs and feathers, painted feathers, and peltry, wrought garters, circlets for the head, girdles. These people dress leather better than any of the other nations, and work in furs and feathers very tastefully, which the Assiniboines are not capable of doing. They are cunning traders, cheating the Assiniboines of all they may possess, such as muskets, powder, balls, kettles, axes, knives or awls. Seeing the great consumption of food daily by the Assiniboines, and afraid that it would not last long, they set afloat a rumour that the Sioux were near and that several of their hunters had noticed them. The Assiniboines fell into the trap and made up their minds quickly to decamp, not wishing to be obliged to fight.

11. THE EXPULSION OF THE ACADIANS (1755).

Source.—A letter sent by Charles Lawrence, Lieut.-Governor of Nova Scotia, to the Governors of the Colonies to which the Acadians were removed : printed in Thomas C. Haliburton's *Historical and Statistical Account of Nova Scotia.* Halifax, 1829.

Halifax, Nova Scotia, 11th Aug., 1755.

Sir,

The success that has attended his Majesty's arms in driving the French out from the encroachments they had made in the Province, furnished me with a favourable opportunity of reducing the French inhabitants of this colony to a proper obedience to his Majesty's Government, or of forcing them to quit the country. These inhabitants were permitted in quiet possession of their lands, upon condition they should take the oath of allegiance to the King within one year after the treaty of Utrecht, by which this Province was ceded to Great Britain ; with this condition they have ever refused to comply without having from the Governor an assurance in writing that they should not be called upon to bear arms in the defence of the Province ; and with this General Philips did comply, of which steps his Majesty has disapproved, and the inhabitants therefrom pretending to be in a state of neutrality between his Majesty and his enemies, have continually furnished the French and Indians with intelligence, quarters, provisions and assistance in annoying the Government; and while one part have abetted the French encroachments by their treachery, the other have countenanced them by open rebellion; and three hundred of them were actually found in arms in the French fort at Beauséjour when it surrendered.

Notwithstanding all their former bad behaviour, as his Majesty was pleased to allow me to extend still further his royal grace to such as would return to their duty, I offered such of them as had not been openly in arms against us a continuance of the possession of their lands, if they would take the oath of allegiance unqualified with any reservation whatever. But this they have audaciously as well as unanimously refused ; and if they would presume to do this when there was a large fleet of ships of war in the harbour and considerable land forces in the Province, what might not we expect from them when the approaching winter deprives us of the former, and when the troops, which are only hired from New England occasionally and for a short time, have returned home ?

As by this behaviour the inhabitants have forfeited all title to their lands and any further favour from the Government, I called together his Majesty's Council, at which the Hon. Vice-Admiral Boscawen and Rear-Admiral Mostyn assisted, to consider by what means we could with the greatest security and effect rid ourselves of a set of people who would for ever have been an obstruction to the intention of settling this colony, and that it was now from their refusal of the oath absolutely incumbent to remove.

As their numbers amount to near seven thousand persons, the driving them off, with leave to go whithersoever they pleased, would have doubtless strengthened Canada with so considerable a number of French inhabitants ; and, as they have no cleared lands to give them at present, such as are able to bear arms must have been immediately employed in annoying this and the neighbouring Colonies. To prevent such an inconveniency, it was judged a necessary and the only practicable measure, to divide them among the Colonies, where they may be of some use, as most of them are healthy strong people, and as they cannot easily collect themselves together again, it will be out of their power to do any mischief, and they may become profitable, and it is possible in time faithful subjects.

As this step was indispensably necessary to the security of the colony, upon whose preservation from French encroachments the prosperity of North America is esteemed in a great measure dependent, I have not the least reason to doubt of your Excellency's concurrence, and that you will receive the inhabitants I now-send, and dispose of them in such a manner as may best answer in preventing their re-union. . . .

12. THE CONQUEST OF CANADA (1757-60).

Source.—*The Letters of Horace Walpole* : edited by Peter Cunningham. Edinburgh, 1906.

8 Sept., 1757. We had a torrent of bad news yesterday from America. Lord Loudon has found an army of twenty-one thousand French, gives over the design on Louisbourg, and retires to Halifax. Admiral Holbourn writes that they have nineteen ships to his seventeen, and he cannot attack them. It is time for England to slip her own cables and float away into some unknown ocean.

24 Aug., 1758. Our next and greatest triumph is the taking of Cape Breton, the account of which came on Friday. The French have not improved like their wines by crossing the sea ; but lost their spirit at Louisbourg as much as on their own coast. The success, especially in the destruction of their fleet, is very great ; the triumphs not at all disproportionate to the conquest, of which you will see all the particulars in the Gazette. Now for the chapter of cypresses. The attempt on Crownpoint has failed ; Lord Howe was killed in a skirmish ; and two days afterward by blunders, rashness and bad intelligence we received a great blow at Ticonderoga. . . . My hope is that Cape Breton may buy us Minorca and a peace.

9 Feb., 1759. The expedition, called to Quebec, departs on Tuesday next under Wolfe and George Townshend, who has thrust himself again into the service, and, as far as wrong-headedness will go, very proper for a hero. Wolfe, who was no friend of Mr. Conway last year and for whom I consequently have no affection, has great merit, spirit and alacrity, and shone extremely at Louisbourg. I am not such a Juno but I will forgive him after eleven more labours.

16 Oct., 1759. I love to prepare your countenance for every event that may happen, for an ambassador, who is nothing but an actor, should be that greatest of actors, a philosopher ; and, with the leave of wise men (that is, hypocrites), philosophy I hold to be little more than presence of mind ; now undoubtedly preparation is a prodigious help to presence of mind. In short, you must not be surprised that we have failed at Quebec, as we certainly shall.[1] You may say, if you please, in the style of modern politics, that your court never supposed it could be taken ; the attempt was only made to draw off the Russians from the King of Prussia, and leave him at liberty to attack Daun. Two days ago came letters from Wolfe, despairing, as much as heroes can despair. The town is well victualled, Amherst is not arrived, and fifteen thousand men encamped defend it. We have lost many men by the enemy, and some by our friends—that is, we now call our nine thousand only seven thousand.

19 Oct. I had no occasion to be in such a hurry to prepare your ambassadorial countenance ; if I had stayed but one day more, I might have left its muscles to behave as they pleased. The notification of a probable disappointment at Quebec came only to heighten the pleasure of the conquest. You may now give yourself what airs you please, you are master of East and West Indies. An ambassador is the only man in the world whom bullying becomes : I beg your pardon, but you are spies, if you are not bragadochios. All precedents are on your side : Persians, Greeks, Romans, always insulted their neighbours when they conquered Quebec. . . .

[1] Cf. Extract 14, pp. 28-30

It was a very singular affair, the generals on both sides slain, and on both sides the second in command wounded ; in short, very near what battles should be, in which only the principals ought to suffer. If their army has not ammunition and spirit enough to fall again upon ours before Amherst comes up, all North America is ours.

21 Oct. Instead of the glorious and ever-memorable year 1759, as the newspapers call it, I call it this ever-warm and victorious year : one would think we had plundered East and West Indies of sunshine. Our bells are worn threadbare with ringing for victories. . . . Adieu ! I don't know a word of news less than the conquest of America.

P.S.—You shall hear from me again if we take Mexico or China before Christmas.

20 June, 1760. Who the deuce was thinking of Quebec ? America was like a book one has read and done with ; or at least if one looked at the book, one just recollected that there was a supplement promised, to contain a chapter on Montreal, the starving and surrender of it—but here are we on a sudden reading our book backwards. An account came two days ago that the French on the march to besiege Quebec had been attacked by General Murray, who got into a mistake and a morass, attacked two bodies that were joined, when he hoped to come up with one of them before the junction, was enclosed, embogged and defeated. By the list of officers killed and wounded, I believe there has been a rueful slaughter,— the place, too, I suppose will be retaken. The year 1760 is not the year 1759.

28 June, 1760. Well, Quebec is come to life again. Last night I went to see the Holdernesses . . . in Sion-lane. As Cibber says of the Revolution, I met the Raising of the Siege ; that is, I met my Lady in a triumphal car, drawn by a Manx horse thirteen little fingers high, with Lady Emily . . . they were going to see the bonfire at the alehouse at the corner. The whole procession returned with me ; and from the

countess's dressing-room, we saw a battery fired before the
house, the mob crying, " God bless the good news ! "

5 Oct., 1760. I am afraid you will turn me off from being
your gazetteer. Do you know that I came to town to-day by
accident, and was here four hours before I heard that Montreal
was taken ? The express came early this morning. I am so
posthumous in my intelligence that you must not expect any
intelligence from me. . . . All I know is, that the bonfires
and squibs are drinking General Amherst's health.

13. THE SIEGE OF QUEBEC (1759).

Source.—A Letter from an Officer to his Friend, quoted in the *Gentleman's Magazine* for December, 1759.

I make no doubt but your anxiety with regard to our
success in this part of the world has been very great, both
with respect to the navigable part (as we were all strangers
and new adventurers) as also for the progress of our troops.
What the French have ever reported of this river is a mere
bugbear, as there are but few dangerous spots in it, and those
very easily discovered ; a proof of their having acted a very
politic part in keeping us so long from attempting to approach
one of the finest countries and climates in the world. The
river abounds with great variety and plenty of fine fish, such
as salmon, sturgeon, bass, cod and all kinds of flat fish. At
the place from which I date this letter the water is entirely
fresh, like that of the Thames, so that we fill all our casks
with it alongside the ship. Great part of the country, from
the isle Bic to Montreal (which is about 25 leagues above
Quebec) is well cultivated, and sowed with wheat, barley, peas,
flax and almost every other kind of grain.
The isle of Orleans is an exceeding fine island, rising very
gradually from the water's edge each way to the middle. It
has many thousand acres of good grain now growing upon it,
and the lands are parted with good paling. It produces great
plenty of French beans, cabbage, turnips and other useful

plants and roots. This island and Coudre the French evacuated at our approach, and left us masters both of their houses and lands ; so that our men were at liberty to pick and choose among fine green peas, currants, gooseberries, apples, raspberries, cherries and, in short, everything of the like kind. This country abounds also with horned cattle, sheep, hogs and poultry ; and in all the woods there is plenty of gooseberries and raspberries uncultivated. Here are numbers of churches, and all kinds of mills round the country. In short, it is a second England, and I am credibly informed the weather is very fine the greatest part of the year.

Quebec is a large city, one part very high, the other at the foot of the eminence. The lower part, containing a large cathedral and Bishop's palace with many other churches, we have reduced to rubbish. Quebec, I assure you, is not that trifling poor fishing town the French have hitherto represented it to be.

The first salutation our ships had on their approach near the town was seven fire-ships well filled with combustibles, and their rigging smeared with tar. These came burning down the river with the help of a strong current, directed on the body of our fleet. But as some such contrivance was expected by the Admiral, good provision was made for his defence by having all the boats of the squadron out, well manned and armed, with an officer in each boat and fire-grapplings. The fire-ships were instantly boarded by our men, who so fixed their grapplings and chains as to tow them clear of every ship to shore on the isle of Orleans, where they burned to ashes without doing the least damage. The next annoyance was 17 fire-rafts, well supplied with gun and pistol barrels loaded, granadoes, and combustibles of all sorts, each of them 103 feet long, and slackly chained together, so that at the least interruption they might surround whatever opposed their passage. They came burning down with the current, and one would have thought the whole river in a flame as they spread almost from shore to shore ; but these were also grappled in like manner, and, being towed clear off all the ships, consumed

with the loss only of one boat, and I believe all the men saved.
General Wolfe, finding so great an opposition, published a
placard and spread it in the French camp ; but it had no
effect on the Canadians ; he therefore ordered all the habitations, barns, stables and corn on the lands, as soon as ripe, to
be totally destroyed. The sides of the river began immediately
to show a most dismal appearance of fire and smoke ; and (as
the troops employed on this service were the remains of those
who escaped the massacre by the French at Fort William
Henry, where they killed and scalped every wounded officer
and common man) they spared little or nothing that came in
their way. Admiral Holmes in the *Sutherland* passed a very
strong battery and went about twenty leagues above the town
in order to burn some frigates and other ships that were got
high up the river. The French pilots themselves were amazed
at the hazards we run with ships of so great burthen, as we
were all higher up the river than any French ships of equal
burthen ever were, above the traverse which their ships scarce
ever passed.

14. WOLFE'S DIFFICULTIES AT QUEBEC (1759).

Source.—Wolfe's Despatch of 2nd September, 1759, quoted in the
Gentleman's Magazine for October, 1759.

. . . The Admiral's despatches and mine would have gone
eight or ten days sooner, if I had not been prevented from
ı writing by a fever. I found myself so ill, and am still so weak,
that I begged the general officers to consult together for the
public utility. They are all of opinion that (as more ships and
provisions have now got above the town) they should try, by
conveying up a corps of 4, or 5000 men (which is nearly the
whole strength of the army, after the points of Lévis and
Orleans are left in a proper state of defence), to draw the
enemy from their present situation and bring them to an
action. I have acquiesced in their proposal, and we are preparing to put it in execution.

The Admiral and I have examined the town with a view to a general assault ; but, after consulting with the chief engineer, who is well acquainted with the interior parts of it, and after viewing it with the utmost attention, we found that, though the batteries of the lower town might be easily silenced by the men-of-war, yet the business of an assault would be little advantaged by that, since the few passages that lead from the lower to the upper town are carefully entrenched ; and the upper batteries cannot be affected by the ships, which must receive considerable damage from them and from the mortars. The Admiral would readily join in this or in any other measure for the public service ; but I could not propose to him an undertaking of so dangerous a nature and promising so little success.

To the uncommon strength of the country, the enemy have added (for the defence of the river) a great number of floating batteries and boats. By the vigilance of these and the Indians round our different posts, it has been impossible to execute anything by surprise. We have had almost daily skirmishes with these savages, in which they are generally defeated, but not without loss on our side.

By the list of disabled officers (many of whom are of rank) you may perceive, Sir, that the army is much weakened. By the nature of the river the most formidable part of this armament is deprived of the power of acting, yet we have almost the whole force of Canada to oppose. In this situation, there is such a choice of difficulties that I own myself at a loss how to determine. The affairs of Great Britain, I know, require the most vigorous measures ; but then the courage of a handful of brave men should be exerted only where there is some hope of a favourable event. However, you may be assured, Sir, that the small part of the campaign which remains shall be employed (as far as I am able) for the honour of his Majesty and the interest of the nation, in which I am sure of being well seconded by the Admiral and by the Generals. Happy if our efforts here can contribute to the success of his Majesty's arms in any other parts of America, I have the honour to be, with the greatest respect, Sir, your most obedient and most humble servant,

JAMES WOLFE.

15. THE PLAINS OF ABRAHAM (1759).

Source.—*An Historical Journal of the Campaigns in North America, 1757-60, by Captain John Knox. London, 1769.*

Thursday, September 13, 1759. Before daybreak this morning we made a descent upon the north shore, about half a quarter of a mile to the eastward of Sillery ; and the light troops were fortunately by the rapidity of the current carried lower down between us and Cape Diamond ; we had in this debarkation thirty flat-bottomed boats containing about sixteen hundred men. This was a great surprise on the enemy, who, from the natural strength of the place, did not suspect, and consequently were not prepared against, so bold an attempt. The chain of sentries which they had posted along the summit of the heights galled us a little and picked off several men and some officers before our light infantry got up to dislodge them. This grand enterprise was conducted and executed with great good order and discretion ; as fast as we landed, the boats put off for reinforcements, and the troops formed with much regularity ; the General with Brigadiers Monckton and Murray were ashore with the first division. We lost no time here, but clambered up one of the steepest precipices that can be conceived, being almost a perpendicular and of an incredible height. As soon as we gained the summit, all was quiet and not a shot was heard owing to the excellent conduct of the light infantry under Colonel Howe ; it was by this time clear daylight. Here we formed again, the river and the south country in our rear, our right extending to the town, our left to Sillery, and halted a few minutes. The General then detached the light troops to our left to rout the enemy from their battery and to disable their guns, except they could be rendered serviceable to the party who were to remain there ; and this service was soon performed. We then

faced to the right and marched towards the town by files till
we came to the plains of Abraham, an even piece of ground
which Mr. Wolfe had made choice of while we stood forming
upon the hill. Weather showery: about six o'clock the
enemy first made their appearance upon the heights between
us and the town; whereupon we halted and wheeled to the
right, thereby forming the line of battle. . . . The enemy
had now likewise formed the line of battle, and got some
cannon to play on us with round and canister shot; but what
galled us most was a body of Indians and other marksmen
they had concealed in the corn opposite to the front of our
right wing and a coppice that stood opposite to our centre
inclining towards our left; but the Colonel Hale, by Brigadier
Monckton's orders, advanced some platoons alternately from
the forty-seventh regiment, which after a few rounds obliged
these skulkers to retire: we were now ordered to lie down,
and remained some time in this position. About eight o'clock
we had two pieces of short brass six-pounders playing on the
enemy, which threw them into some confusion, and obliged
them to alter their disposition, and Montcalm formed them
into three large columns; about nine the two armies moved
a little nearer each other. The light cavalry made a faint
attempt upon our parties at the battery of Sillery, but were
soon beat off, and Monsieur de Bougainville with his troops
from Cape Rouge came down to attack the flank of our second
line, hoping to penetrate there; but by a masterly disposition
of Brigadier Townshend they were forced to desist, and the
third battalion of Royal Americans was then detached to the
first ground we had formed on after we gained the heights,
to preserve the communication with the beach and our boats.
About ten o'clock the enemy began to advance briskly in
three columns with loud shouts and recovered arms, two of
them inclining to the left of our army and the third towards
our right, firing obliquely at the two extremities of our line
from the distance of one hundred and thirty until they came
within forty yards; which our troops withstood with the
greatest intrepidity and firmness, still reserving their fire and

paying the strictest obedience to their officers ; this uncommon
steadiness, together with the havoc which the grape-shot from
our field-pieces made among them, threw them into some disorder and was most critically maintained by a well-timed,
regular, and heavy discharge of our small arms, such as they
could no longer oppose ; hereupon they gave way and fled
with precipitation, so that by the time the cloud of smoke
was vanished our men were again loaded, and profiting by
the advantage we had over them pursued them almost to the
gates of the town and the bridge over the little river, re-
doubling our fire with great eagerness, making many officers
and men prisoners. The weather cleared up, with a comfort-
ably warm sunshine ; the Highlanders chased them vigorously
towards Charles's river, and the fifty-eighth to the suburb
close to John's gate, until they were checked by the cannon
from the two hulks ; at the same time a gun, which the town
had brought to bear upon us with grape-shot, galled the
progress of the regiments to the right, who were likewise
pursuing with equal ardour, while Colonel Hunt Walsh by a
very judicious movement wheeled the battalions of Bragg and
Kennedy to the left, and flanked the coppice where a body of
the enemy made a stand, as if willing to renew the action ;
but a few platoons from these corps completed our victory.
Then it was that Brigadier Townshend came up, called off
the pursuers, ordered the whole line to dress and recover their
former ground. Our joy at this success is inexpressibly damped
by the loss we sustained of one of the greatest heroes which
this or any other age can boast of,—GENERAL JAMES WOLFE,
who received his mortal wound, as he was exerting himself
at the head of the grenadiers of Louisbourg. . . . The officers
who are prisoners say that Quebec will surrender in a few days :
some deserters, who came out to us in the evening, agree in
that opinion, and inform us that the Sieur de Montcalm is
dying in great agony of a wound he received to-day in their
retreat.

Source.—The Letter in the *Gentleman's Magazine*, December, 1759, already quoted (13).

[Wolfe was wounded three times.] He then went reeling aside, but was soon supported by an officer, of whom he inquired if the enemy were put to flight ; and, being assured they were, and that our troops were in pursuit, he smiled and said he died with pleasure on the spot he ever wished to die on, and then closed his eyes. Thus died this great young General, whose behaviour on this day will ever be an honour to his country. . . .

'Tis an oble summer's work, though many brave fellows have suffered much by it ; but all, both soldiers and sailors, to a man behaved nobly. The French army consisted of about 5000 regulars, the rest Canadians, some of very considerable fortune, many of whom fell in the action, and the rest are reduced almost to beggary. The prisoners all agree that this is the greatest stroke the French ever felt from the English arms ; and I readily believe it, as the place is incredibly strong, and by its surrender we must make North America our own.

16. GOVERNMENT OF QUEBEC UNDER THE BRITISH (1763-74).

Source.—The Proclamation of 7th October, 1763, printed in *Documents relating to the Constitutional History of Canada*, 1759-91, edited by Adam Shortt and Arthur G. Doughty.

WHEREAS we have taken into Our Royal Consideration the extensive and valuable Acquisitions in America, secured to our Crown by the late Definitive Treaty of Peace, concluded at Paris, the 10th Day of February last ; and being desirous that all Our loving Subjects, as well of our Kingdom as of our Colonies in America, may avail themselves with all convenient Speed, of the great Benefits and Advantages which must accrue therefrom to their Commerce, Manufactures and Navigation, We have thought fit, with the Advice of our Privy

Council, to issue this our Royal Proclamation, hereby to publish and declare to all our loving Subjects, that we have, with the advice of our said Privy Council, granted our Letters Patent, under our Great Seal of Great Britain, to erect, within the Countries and Islands ceded and confirmed to Us by the said Treaty, Four distinct and separate Governments, styled and called by the names of Quebec, East Florida, West Florida and Grenada. . . .

And whereas it will greatly contribute to the speedy settling our said new Governments, that our loving subjects should be informed of our Paternal care, for the security of the Liberties and Properties of those who are and shall become Inhabitants thereof, We have thought fit to publish and declare . . . that we have . . . given express Power and Direction to our Governors of our said Colonies respectively, that so soon as the state and circumstances of the said Colonies will admit thereof, they shall, with the Advice and Consent of the Members of our Council, summon and call General Assemblies within the said Governments respectively, in such Manner and Form as is used and directed in those Colonies and Provinces in America which are under our immediate Government ; and We have also given Power to the said Governors, with the consent of our said Councils and the Representatives of the People so to be summoned as aforesaid, to make, constitute, and ordain Laws, Statutes, and Ordinances for the Public Peace, Welfare, and good Government of our said Colonies, and of the People and Inhabitants thereof, as near as may be agreeable to the Laws of England, and under such Regulations and Restrictions as are used in other Colonies ; and in the mean Time, and until such Assemblies can be called as aforesaid, all Persons Inhabiting in or resorting to our said Colonies may confide in our Royal Protection for the Enjoyment of the Benefit of the Laws of our Realm of England ; for which Purpose We have given Power under our Great Seal to the Governors of our said Colonies respectively to erect and constitute, with the Advice of our said Councils respectively, Courts of Judicature and public Justice within our said Colonies for hearing and determining all Causes, as well Criminal as Civil, according to Law and Equity, and as near as may be agreeable to the Laws of England, with Liberty to all Persons who may think themselves aggrieved by the Sentences of such Courts, in all Civil Cases, to appeal, under the usual Limitations and Restrictions, to Us in our Privy Council.

17. ON THE COPPERMINE RIVER IN JULY (1771).

Source.—Samuel Hearne's *A Journey from Prince of Wales Fort in Hudson's Bay to the Northern Ocean*. London, 1795.

After a sleep of five or six hours we once more set out, and walked eighteen or nineteen miles to the South South East, when we arrived at one of the copper mines, which lies, from the river's mouth about South South East, distant about twenty-nine or thirty miles.

This mine, if it deserve that appellation, is no more than an entire jumble of rocks and gravel, which has been rent many ways by an earthquake. Through these ruins there runs a small river ; but no part of it, at the time I was there, was more than knee-deep.

The Indians who were the occasion of my undertaking this journey, represented this mine to be so rich and valuable, that if a factory were built at the river, a ship might be ballasted with the ore, instead of stone ; and that with the same ease and dispatch as is done with stones at Churchill River. By their account the hills were entirely composed of that metal, all in handy lumps, like a heap of pebbles. But their account differed so much from the truth, that I and almost all my companions expended near four hours in search of some of this metal, with such poor success, that among us all only one piece of any size could be found. This, however, was remarkably good, and weighed above four pounds. I believe the copper has formerly been in much greater plenty ; for in many places, both on the surface and in the cavities and crevices of the rocks, the stones are much tinged with verdigris.

It may not be unworthy the notice of the curious, or un-deserving a place in my Journal, to remark that the Indians imagine that every bit of copper they find resembles some object in nature; but, by what I saw of the large piece, and some smaller ones which were found by my companions, it requires a great share of invention to make this out. I found that different people had different ideas on the subject, for the large piece of copper above mentioned had not been found long before it had twenty different names . . . at last it was generally allowed to resemble an Alpine hare couchant: for my part, I must confess that I could not see it had the least resemblance to any thing to which they compared it. . . .

Before Churchill River was settled by the Hudson's Bay Company, which was not more than fifty years previous to this journey being undertaken, the Northern Indians had no other metal but copper among them, except a small quantity of iron-work, which a party of them who visited York Fort about the year 1713 or 1714 purchased; and a few pieces of old iron found at Churchill River, which had undoubtedly been left there by Captain Monk. This being the case, numbers of them from all quarters used every summer to resort to these hills in search of copper; of which they made hatchets, ice-chisels, bayonets, knives, awls, arrow-heads, etc. The many paths that had been beaten by the Indians on these occasions, and which are yet, in many places, very perfect, especially on the dry ridges and hills, is surprising; in the valleys and marshy grounds, however, they are mostly grown over with herbage, so as not to be discerned.

The Copper Indians set a great value on their native metal even to this day; and prefer it to iron for almost every use except that of a hatchet, a knife, and an awl; for these three necessary implements copper makes but a very poor substitute.

18· THE QUEBEC ACT (1774).

Source.—Shortt and Doughty's *Constitutional Documents* (*cf.* 16).

. . . for the more perfect security and ease of the minds of the inhabitants of the said province, it is hereby declared, that his Majesty's subjects professing the religion of the Church of Rome of and in the said province of Quebec, may have, hold and enjoy the free exercise of the religion of the Church of Rome, subject to the King's supremacy . . . and that the clergy of the said Church may hold, receive and enjoy their accustomed dues and rights, with respect to such persons only as shall profess the said religion. . . .

. . . all his Majesty's Canadian subjects within the province of Quebec, the religious Orders and Communities only excepted, may also hold and enjoy their property and possessions, together with all customs and usages relative thereto, and all other their civil rights, in as large, ample and beneficial manner . . . as may consist with their allegiance to his Majesty, and subjection to the Crown and Parliament of Great Britain; and . . . in all matters of controversy relative to property and civil rights, resort shall be had to the laws of Canada as the rule for the decision of the same. . . .

And whereas the certainty and lenity of the Criminal Law of England, and the benefits and advantages resulting from the use of it, have been sensibly felt by the inhabitants, from an experience of more than nine years, during which it has been uniformly administered ; be it therefore further enacted . . . that the same shall continue to be administered, and shall be observed as law in the province of Quebec. . . .

And whereas it may be necessary to ordain many regulations for the future welfare and good government of the province of Quebec, the occasions of which cannot now be foreseen, nor, without much delay and inconvenience, be provided for, without entrusting that authority, for a certain time and under proper restrictions, to persons resident there : And whereas it is at present inexpedient to call an Assembly . . . it shall and may be lawful for his Majesty . . . to constitute and appoint a Council for the affairs of the province of Quebec, to consist of such persons resident there, not exceeding twenty-three nor less than seventeen, as his Majesty . . . shall be pleased to appoint . . . which Council, so appointed and nominated, or the major part thereof, shall have power and authority to make ordinances for the peace, welfare and good government of the said province, with the consent of his Majesty's Governor, or, in his absence, of the Lieutenant-Governor or Commander-in-Chief for the time being.

19. ONE OF THE LOYALISTS (1783).

Source.—A Memoir by his Grand-daughter, Mrs. Sophia Rowe, in the *Transactions* for 1899 of The United Empire Loyalists' Association of Ontario.

The late Captain Samuel Anderson was born of Irish parents near Boston on 4th of May, 1736. He was a lawyer in good practice and married Miss Prudentia Deliverance Butts of Boston, who was born 1743 and died 1824. Samuel Anderson went to the West Indies early in life for the benefit of his health. On his return he joined the King's forces, probably as one of the contingent furnished by the New England Provinces after the breaking out of the war with France in 1756. He served under General Abercrombie in 1758, and under General Amherst in 1759-60-61. . . . After the close of the war, he settled on a farm near Boston, where he resided until the breaking out of the rebellion in 1775. He was offered a company in the Continental Service, which he refused. Some time after, he was offered command of a regiment in the same service, which he also refused. This caused him to be looked upon as a *King's Man* and led to an attempt on the part of some of his neighbours to convert him from the error of his ways by one or other of the gentle means of carting, flogging, or tar-and-feathering then in vogue amongst the revolutionary party. Five or six of them started out to try the experiment; they found him on his farm splitting rails; he politely asked them their business, and, on being told they had come to teach him a lesson, he invited them to " come and try." As he was a very large and powerful man, they looked at him, then at the axe in his hand, and moved off, evidently considering " discretion the better part of valour." Several attempts were made to arrest him, and he was at one time secreted on his own property, when a party of Continentals billeted themselves at his house. The sergeant read a proclamation offering a reward of five hundred pounds for the body of Samuel Anderson dead or alive, after which the party conversed in French, not thinking they would be understood by Mrs. Anderson ; but the brave woman, without betraying the slightest fear or knowledge of what they talked of, heard all they purposed doing to her husband, should he be found. She directed her servants to prepare food and beds for all, had their horses stabled and fed, then, waiting till all was quiet, went in the dark to her husband and bade him fly for his life.

However, he with many other loyalists were captured and confined in Litchfield jail, where they suffered all but death until the beginning of 1777, when, having been told that all the prisoners were to be shot the next day, Anderson wrenched the bars from a window, and with his companions escaped to Canada, where he was appointed a Captain in the 1st Battalion of Sir John Johnston's corps, the King's Royal Regiment of New York. When General Burgoyne was preparing to advance from Ticonderoga, Captain Anderson was placed at the head of the workmen who were employed in making the roads through the forest from the head of Lake Champlain towards Fort Edward. He served in the battalion of the Royal Yorkers until they were disbanded in the spring of 1784. From the time of his imprisonment in Litchfield jail, his wife saw nothing of him until late in 1778, when, after suffering terribly from the cruelty of the Continentals, she abandoned all her property, paid the Yankee Governor 2s. 6d. for a pass, and with her family made her way to Sorel, where her husband was then stationed with his company of the Royal Yorkers, where they remained till the spring of 1783, when he with his two elder sons who had served under him were put on half pay when peace was declared ; and at the reduction of the army, Anderson, with his family and the men of his company, received their allotment of lands in Cornwall, then a wilderness, the nearest settlement being Montreal distant 68 miles, and Kingston 105 miles. They came up the St. Lawrence by batteaux, and lived for some time under shelter of cedar boughs, until able to erect log houses for themselves. A short time after their arrival the " Dark Sunday " occurred, when at mid-day total darkness fell upon all the land, and continued for about two hours. The rain came down in torrents, flooding their temporary dwelling, causing great discomfort, while the thunder and lightning were terrific. In those days there were no merchants, no baker or butcher shops, no medical men, no ministers to console the sick or dying or bury the dead, and no means of instruction for the young. The Loyalists were generally poor, having sacrificed their property to their politics, and were obliged to work very hard. All was bush, hard labour and pinching privation for the present and long toil for the rising generation. The only mail in the early settlement of West Canada between Kingston and Montreal was in the winter carried three times by an old French Canadian, Jacques Morriseau, who travelled the whole distance on snow shoes. His food was sea biscuit and fat pork which he ate and enjoyed sitting on a snow bank, and would afterwards puff away dull care in clouds of smoke curling from his old clay pipe, the stem of which was just long enough to keep the burning punk with which he lit it about two inches from his nose. From Lachine to Cornwall, he was obliged to sleep out of doors three nights—the settlers were then so few and far between, he could not always reach a house—and the only bed he had on these occasions was of green boughs under him and a blanket to cover him. He always rested a night going either way under Captain Anderson's roof. In 1785, Captain Anderson was appointed a magistrate . . . and drew half pay as a Captain until his death, which occurred in June, 1836 (born 1736), not from any bodily ailment, but accidentally falling, his hip joint was broken, and from his great age the bones would not unite.

20. THE DESCENT OF THE MACKENZIE RIVER (1789).

Source.—Sir Alexander Mackenzie's *Voyages from Montreal through the Continent of North America to the Frozen and Pacific Oceans in the years* 1789 *and* 1793. London, 1801.

5 July, 1789. . . . There were five families, consisting of twenty-five or thirty persons, and of two different tribes, the Slave and Dog-rib Indians. We made them smoke, though it was evident they did not know the use of tobacco ; we likewise supplied them with grog ; but I am disposed to think that they accepted our civilities rather from fear than inclination. We acquired a more effectual influence over them by the distribution of knives, beads, awls, rings, gartering, fire-steels, flints and hatchets ; so that they became more familiar even than we expected, for we could not keep them out of our tents ; though I did not observe that they attempted to purloin anything.

The information which they gave respecting the river had so much of the fabulous that I shall not detail it : it will be sufficient just to mention their attempts to persuade us that it would require several winters to get to the sea, and that old age would come upon us before the period of our return : we were also to encounter monsters of such horrid shapes and destructive powers as could only exist in their wild imaginations. They added, besides, that there were two impassable falls in the river, the first of which was about thirty days march from us.

Though I placed no faith in these strange relations, they had a very different effect upon our Indians, who were already tired of the voyage. It was their opinion and anxious wish that we should not hesitate to return. They said that, according to the information which they had received, there were very few animals in the country beyond us, and that, as we proceeded, the scarcity would increase, and we should absolutely perish from hunger, if no other accident befell us. It was with no small trouble that they were convinced of the folly of these reasonings ; and, by my desire, they induced one of those Indians to accompany us, in consideration of a small kettle, an axe, a knife, and some other articles.

Though it was now three o'clock in the afternoon, the canoe was ordered to be reloaded, and, as we were ready to embark, our new recruit was desired to prepare himself for his departure, which he would have declined ; but as none of his friends would take his place, we may be said, after the delay of an hour, to have compelled him to embark. Previous to his departure a ceremony took place, of which I could not learn the meaning ; he cut off a lock of his hair, and having divided it into three parts, he fastened one of them to the hair on the upper part of his wife's head, blowing on it three times with the utmost violence in his power, and uttering certain words. The other two he fastened with the same formalities on the heads of his two children.

During our short stay with these people, they amused us with dancing, which they accompanied with their voices ; but neither their song or their dance possessed much variety. The men and women formed a promiscuous ring. The former have a bone dagger or piece of stick between the fingers of the right hand, which they keep extended above the head, in continual motion ; the left they seldom raise so high, but work it backwards and forwards in an horizontal direction ; while they leap about and throw themselves into various antic postures, to the measure of their music, always bringing their heels close to each other at every pause. The men occasionally howl in imitation of some animal, and he who continues this violent exercise for the longest period, appears to be considered as the best performer.

21. THE CONSTITUTIONAL ACT OF 1791.

Source.—Shortt and Doughty's *Documents*. (Cf. 16.)

II. . . . whereas his Majesty has been pleased to signify by his message to both Houses of Parliament, his royal intention to divide his province of Quebec into two separate provinces, to be called *The Province of Upper Canada* and *The Province of Lower Canada* . . . there shall be within each of the said provinces respectively a Legislative Council and an Assembly. . . .

III. . . . it shall and may be lawful for his Majesty . . . to authorise and direct the Governor or Lieutenant-Governor . . . to summon to the said Legislative Council . . . a sufficient number of discreet and proper persons, being not fewer than seven to the Legislative Council for the province of Upper Canada, and not fewer than fifteen to the Legislative Council for the province of Lower Canada. . . .

XIV. . . . for the purpose of electing the members of such Assemblies respectively, it shall and may be lawful for his Majesty . . . to authorise the Governor or Lieutenant-Governor . . . to issue a proclamation dividing such province into districts or counties or circles, and towns or townships, and appointing the limits thereof, and declaring and appointing the number of representatives to be chosen by each of such districts. . . .

XVII. . . . the whole number of members to be chosen in the province of Upper Canada shall not be less than sixteen, . . . in the province of Lower Canada shall not be less than fifty.

XXVII. . . . the said Legislative Council and Assembly, in each of the said provinces, shall be called together once at the least in every twelve calendar months, and . . . every Assembly shall continue for four years . . . subject nevertheless to be sooner prorogued or dissolved by the Governor. . . .

XXX. . . . whenever any bill which has been passed by the Legislative Council and by the House of Assembly . . . shall be presented, for his Majesty's assent, to the Governor

. . . such Governor . . . is hereby authorised and required to declare, according to his discretion, but subject nevertheless to the provisions contained in this Act, and to such instructions as may from time to time be given in that behalf by his Majesty . . . that he assents to such bill in his Majesty's name, or that he witholds his Majesty's assent from such bill, or that he reserves such bill for the signification of his Majesty's pleasure thereon.

XXXI. . . . whenever any bill . . . shall by such Governor . . . have been assented to in his Majesty's name, such Governor . . . is hereby required, by the first convenient opportunity, to transmit to one of his Majesty's principal Secretaries of State an authentic copy of such bill so assented to ; . . . it shall and may be lawful, at any time within two years after such bill shall have been so received . . . for his Majesty . . . to declare his . . . disallowance of such bill. . . .

XXXVI. . . . it shall and may be lawful for his Majesty . . . to authorise the Governor . . . to make, from and out of the lands of the Crown within such provinces, such allotment and appropriation of lands, for the support and maintenance of a Protestant clergy within the same, as may bear a due proportion to the amount of such lands within the same as have at any time been granted by or under the authority of his Majesty ; . . . such lands so allotted and appropriated shall be, as nearly as the circumstances and nature of the case will admit, of the like quality as the lands in respect of which the same are so allotted . . . and shall be, as nearly as the same can be estimated at the time of making such grant, equal in value to the seventh part of the lands so granted.

XLIII. . . . all lands which shall be hereafter granted within the said province of Upper Canada shall be granted in free and common soccage, in like manner as lands are now holden in free and common soccage in that part of Great Britain called England ; . . . in every case where lands shall be hereafter granted within the said province of Lower Canada, and where the grantee thereof shall desire the same to be granted in free and common soccage, the same shall be so granted ; but subject nevertheless to such alterations, with respect to the nature and consequences of such tenure of free and common soccage, as may be established by any law or laws which may be made by his Majesty . . . by and with the advice and consent of the Legislative Council and Assembly of the province.

XLVI. . . . nothing in this Act shall extend . . . to prevent or affect the execution of any law which hath been or shall at any time be made by his Majesty . . . and the Parliament of Great Britain, for establishing regulations of prohibitions, or for imposing, levying or collecting duties for the regulation of navigation, or for the regulation of the commerce to be carried on between the said two provinces or between either of the said provinces and any foreign country or state, or for appointing and directing the payment of drawbacks of such duties so imposed. . . .

22.   TO THE PACIFIC OVERLAND.   THE FIRST CROSSING OF NORTH AMERICA NORTH OF MEXICO (1793).

Source.—Sir A. Mackenzie's *Voyages*. (Cf. 20.)

Sunday, 21 July, 1793. . . . We landed, and found the ruins of a village, in a situation calculated for defence. The place itself was overgrown with weeds, and in the centre of the houses there was a temple of the same form and construction as that which I described at the large village. We were soon followed by ten canoes, each of which contained from three to six men. They informed us that we were expected at the village, where we should see many of them. From their general deportment I was very apprehensive that some hostile design was meditated against us, and for the first time I acknowledged my apprehensions to my people. I accordingly desired them to be very much upon their guard, and to be prepared if any violence was offered to defend themselves to the last.

We had no sooner landed than we took possession of a rock, where there was not space for more than twice our number, and which admitted of our defending ourselves with advantage, in case we should be attacked. The people in the three first canoes were the most troublesome, but, after doing their utmost to irritate us, they went away. They were, however, no sooner gone than an hat, an handkerchief and several other articles were missing. The rest of our visitors continued their pressing invitations to accompany them to their village, but finding our resolution to decline them was not to be shaken, they about sunset relieved us from all further importunities by their departure. . . .

The natives having left us, we made a fire to warm ourselves, and as for supper there was but little of that, for our whole daily allowance did not amount to what was sufficient for a single meal. The weather was clear throughout the day, which was succeeded by a fine moonlight night. I directed the people to keep watch by two in turn, and laid myself down in my cloak.

Monday, 22nd. This morning the weather was clear and pleasant ; nor had anything occurred to disturb us throughout the night. One solitary Indian, indeed, came to us with about half a pound of boiled seal's flesh and the head of a small salmon, for which he asked an handkerchief, but afterwards accepted a few beads. As this man came alone, I concluded that no general plan had been formed among the natives to annoy us, but this opinion did not altogether calm the apprehensions of my people. . . .

Two canoes now arrived from the same quarter as the rest with several men and our young Indian along with them. They brought a very few small sea-otter skins out of season, with some pieces of raw seal's flesh. The former were of no value, but hunger compelled some of my people to take the latter at an extravagant price. Mr. Mackay lighted a bit of touchwood with a burning-glass in the cover of his tobacco-box, which so surprised the natives that they exchanged the best of their otter-skins for it. The young man was now very anxious to persuade our people to depart, as the natives, he said, were as numerous as mosquitoes and of very malignant character. This information produced some very earnest remonstrances to me to hasten our departure, but, as I was determined not to leave this place, except I was absolutely compelled to it, till I had ascertained its situation,[1] these solicitations were not repeated.

While I was taking a meridian, two canoes of a larger size and well-manned appeared from the main South-West channel. They seemed to be the forerunners of others who were coming to co-operate with the people of the village . . . and our young Indian, who understood them, renewed his entreaties for our departure, as they would soon come to shoot their arrows and hurl their spears at us. In relating our danger, his agitation was so violent that he foamed at the mouth. . . . The two canoes now approached the shore, and in a short time five men with their families landed very quietly from them. My instruments being exposed, they examined them with much apparent admiration and astonishment. . . .

I now mixed up some vermilion in melted grease, and inscribed in large characters on the South-East face of the rock on which we had slept last night this brief memorial : "Alexander Mackenzie from Canada by land, the twenty-second of July, one thousand seven hundred and ninety-three."

As I thought that we were too near the village, I consented to leave the place, and accordingly proceeded North-East three miles, when we landed on a point in a small cove, where we should not be readily seen and could not be attacked except in our front.

[1] Mackenzie found his situation to be on an arm of "Vancouver's Cascade Canal," part of what is now Burke Channel, about 52° 20' N. lat.

23. A SERVANT OF THE NORTH-WEST COMPANY (1800).

Source.—The Journal of James M'Kenzie in the Athabasca District, printed in *Les Bourgeois de la Compagnie du Nord-Ouest*, by L. R. Masson. Quebec, 1890.

16 Jan. This morning, Charles Cadien's comrade arrived and paid 62 skins. . . . He was so haughty on his arrival on account of his skins that he threw the tobacco I gave him in my face, saying it was not good, and that I lied when I said there was none better in the fort. The men's advice, though not asked, was to pack the piece of tobacco into the Indian's nose, or give him a kicking for his bad breeding. . . . This rough usage I thought bad encouragement for him to kill more beaver, and a very indifferent recompense for those he had already brought, which I think made ample amends for his insults. However, in case he might do the like again, perhaps when he had no such substantial atonement to offer, I told him to take care and not behave so impudently in future. . . .

17 Feb. It is unnecessary telling always in the journal that every Indian who arrives, whether good, bad, or indifferent, gets a bit of tobacco and a dram ; it suffices to tell once that it is the custom of the place ; and any one who reads of an Indian's arrival may suppose that this custom is followed, and, should he wish to know how many bits of tobacco and drams were expended, he can count the Montagners on his fingers as he reads on ; the number of Montagners found will be the number of the bits of tobacco and drams required. If he wishes to know the real value given, I will tell him, the tobacco is always rotten and the rum mostly water. . . .

28 March. Sent Marlin 15 measures mixed rum and 3 feet tobacco. Now, for you, Antitheses Philosophers, who are for ever moved by the spirit of contradiction and feel an itching to find fault where there is none, here is a fine occasion to show your wonderful parts and produce something worthy of your sect. Sending rum to the Indians, according to you, is an

unpardonable error in a poor fellow's conduct ; but may he beg leave, Gentlemen, to ask you a few plain questions by way of vindication of his supposed error ?   Pray then ! will 19 packs of fine beaver have no weight in your debates ? If they will not, I am sure they will in the Gentlemen of the North-West Company's pockets, when reduced into hard cash.

What is the reason you fret so much about sending rum to the Indians more than other goods ? Is it because 7 parts of the 8 of this rum are pure water, of course, less expensive to the Company and more pleasing to the Indians than other goods ? No, Gentlemen, I suppose you will say it is because it debauches the Indians and renders them troublesome. . . .

If the Indians be spoiled, it is the *Bourgeois* and not the clerks that do it ; the former give the Indians every time they pass large presents, which the latter are either afraid or forbidden to give ; the one, in consequence, is regarded by the Indians as a superior being whom they must respect, the other is a mere tool to them whom they despise and need not mind. . . .

Here again, Gentlemen of the " Critic Class," you will reprimand my warmth, which in your opinion is impertinence, to presume to speak against my employers, but be pleased to recollect that, though I have spoken against some of their actions, yet I have not against their interests.

24. THE BEAVER (1807).

Source.—*Travels through the Canadas*, by George Heriot, Deputy Post-master-General of British North America. London, 1807.

The beavers associate in bands to the number of about an hundred in each, and are supposed, by several who have witnessed their economy, to possess a certain jargon, by means of which they communicate their sentiments to each other. Certain it is, that they have a mode of consulting together respecting the construction of their cabins, their dykes, their artificial lakes, and many other things which concern the preservation and safety of their republic. They are said to station

sentinels, whilst they are occupied in cutting down with their
teeth trees as large in circumference as casks, on the borders
of the lakes; and these sentinels, by a cry or by knocking
their tail against the surface of the water, give warning of the
approach of men or animals, when the others instantly for-
sake their labours, and, plunging into the water, save themselves by swimming to their cabins.

When beavers have made choice of a meadow traversed by
a rivulet, they construct, by their joint operation, dams or
causeways, which, impeding the course of the water, produce
an inundation over the whole meadow, sometimes several
leagues in circumference. The dam is composed of trees, which
these animals cut down with their four incisive teeth, drag
along through the water, and arrange across the river in the
situation most convenient for stopping its course. They afterwards bring grass, small wood and clay in their mouths and
on their tails, which they deposit between the wood with so
much industry and art, that a wall of masonry of greater
strength could scarcely be constructed. They labour during
the night with diligence and perseverance. Their tails supply
the want of trowels, their teeth serve them for axes, and their
forefeet for hands. Dykes, two or three hundred feet in length,
twenty feet high, and seven or eight in thickness, are thus
completed in the space of five or six months, although not
more than a hundred of these little animals have assisted
each other in the operation. The savages never destroy these
dykes, but, from a principle of superstition, allow them to
remain entire, and are satisfied with making only a small
passage for the draining of the water. Besides the faculty
which the beavers possess of cutting down trees, the judgment
which they have acquired in directing the fall of these immense
masses upon the water, appears still more singular. They pay
attention to the direction of the wind, and carry on the process
in such a manner as to derive aid from thence, and thereby to
ensure the falling of the tree upon a lake or across a rivulet.

The neatness and convenience of their habitations seem to
evince a greater portion of skill and ingenuity than even the

dykes, both strength and address being necessary to enable them to plant six stakes in the bed of the water. These are arranged exactly in the centre of the pond, and upon them their house is erected in the form of an oven, being composed of clay, of grass and of branches of trees, to the height of three ￫ stages, in order to possess a retreat, by ascending from one to the other when the waters are increased by inundations, caused by the melting of the ice and snows. The floors are made of junks of trees, and each beaver has a distinct apartment. The entrance is from beneath the water, where a large hole is made in the first floor, surrounded by tender branches cut into small pieces, that they may be more easily drawn into the cells when they are inclined to eat ; for, as these constitute their principal food, they have the foresight to lay in a great store, particularly in autumn, before the frosts congeal their lake and confine them to their cabins for two or three months.

The precaution which they use to establish and maintain order in their republic, and to guard against pursuit, is admirable. All other animals upon earth, however strong, however swift, vigorous and armed by nature, stand in awe of creatures that are capable of injuring them. The beaver, however, seems to have no other foe than man to apprehend. The wolves, the foxes, and the bears, are little solicitous to attack it in its cabin ; had they even the faculty of diving, they would not find the event greatly to their profit, for the beaver, with his incisory and penetrating teeth, is capable of maintaining a formidable defence.

The beavers are seldom taken in snares, unless they are baited with a species of willow which is rare and of which they are very fond. The mode of taking them in autumn is ￫ by making a hole of three or four feet in diameter in the foundation of the dyke, to draw off the water, and the beavers being left dry, the savages find them an easy prey. . . .

In winter, when the waters are frozen, they make holes in the ice around the lodges of the beavers, to which nets are fixed from the one to the other, and when they are properly extended, they uncover with axes the cabins of these poor animals, which, throwing themselves into the water and returning to breathe at the holes, are entangled in the snares, from whence none escape but such as the savages are inclined to exempt from the general havoc.

25. A RAPID ON THE FRASER RIVER (1808).

Source.—Simon Fraser's "Journal" of the First Descent of the River, printed in Masson's *Bourgeois du Nord-Ouest*. Quebec, 1889-90.

21 June. Soon after we were alarmed by the loud bawling of our guides whom we saw running full speed towards us and making signs that our people were lost in the rapid. As we could not account for this misfortune, we immediately ran over to the baggage where we found Mr. Quesnel all alone. We inquired of him about the men; at the same time we discovered that three of the canoes were missing, but he had seen none of them, nor did he know where they were. On casting our view across the river, we remarked one of the canoes and some of the men ashore there. From this incident we had reason to believe that the others were either ahead or had perished. We immediately directed our speed to the lower end of the rapid. . . .

We had not proceeded far when we observed one of our men, Dalaire, walking slowly from the bank with a stick in his hand, and, on coming up to him, we discovered that he was so wet, so weak and exhausted that he could scarcely speak. However, after leaning a little while on his stick and recovering his breath, he informed us that unfortunately he and the others, finding the carrying place too long and the canoes too heavy, took it upon themselves to venture down by water; that the canoe in which he was happened to be the last in setting out.

"In the first cascade," said he, "our canoe filled and upset; the foreman and the steersman got on the outside, but I, who was in the centre, remained a long while underneath upon the bars; the canoe still drifting was thrown into a smoothy current and the other two men finding an opportunity sprang from their situation into the water and swam ashore. The impulse occasioned by their weight in leaping off raised one side of the canoe above the surface, and, having still my recollection though I had swallowed a quantity of water, I seized the critical moment to disentangle myself, and I gained, though not without a struggle, the top of the canoe. By this time I found myself again in the middle of the stream ; here I continued astride the canoe, humouring the tide as well as I could with my body to preserve my balance, and, although I scarcely had time to look about me, I had the satisfaction to observe the two other canoes ashore near an eddy and their crews safe among the rocks.

" In the second or third cascade (for I do not recollect which), the canoe plunged from a great height into an eddy below, and striking with great violence against the bottom split in two. Here I lost my recollection, which, however, I soon recovered, and was surprised to find myself on a smooth, easy current, with only one half of the canoe in my arms. In this condition I continued through several cascades until the stream carried me into an eddy at the foot of a high and steep rock. Here, my strength being exhausted, I lost my hold, a large wave washed me from off the wreck among the rocks and another still larger hoisted me clear on shore, where I remained, you readily believe, some time motionless. At length, recovering a little of my strength, I crawled up among the rocks and found myself once more safe on firm ground, just as you see."

Here he finished his melancholy tale, then pointed to the place of his landing which we went to see and were lost in astonishment, not only at his escape from the waves, but also at his courage and perseverance in effecting a passage up through a place which appeared to us a perfect precipice. Continuing our course along the bank, we found that he had drifted three miles among rapids, cascades, whirlpools, etc., all inconceivably dangerous. . . .

Some time after, upon advancing towards the camp, we picked up all the men on our side of the river ; the men who had been thrown ashore on the other side joined us in the evening. They informed us that the Indians assisted greatly in extricating them from their difficulties ; indeed, the Indians showed us every possible attention during our misfortune on this trying occasion.

26. LAURA SECORD, JUNE, 1813.

Source.—Her Own Narrative in the *Anglo-American Magazine*, Toronto, November, 1853 : quoted in *The Documentary History of the Campaigns upon the Niagara Frontier*, edited for the Lundy's Lane Historical Society by Lieut.-Col. E. Cruikshank.

I shall commence at the battle of Queenston, where I was at the time the cannon balls were flying around me in every direction. I left the place during the engagement. After the battle I returned to Queenston, and there found that my husband had been wounded, my house plundered and property destroyed. It was while the Americans had possession of the frontier that I learned the plans of the American commander and determined to put the British troops under FitzGibbon in possession of them, and if possible to save the British troops from capture or perhaps total destruction. In doing so I found I should have great difficulty in getting through the American guards, which were out ten miles in the country. Determined to persevere, I left early in the morning, walked nineteen miles in the month of June over a rough and difficult part of the country, when I came to a field belonging to a Mr. Decamp in the neighbourhood of the Beaver Dam. By this time daylight had left me. Here I found all the Indians encamped ; by moonlight the scene was terrifying and to those accustomed to such scenes might be considered grand. Upon advancing to the Indians they all rose and with some yells said, " Woman," which made me tremble. I cannot express the awful feeling it gave me, but I did not lose my presence of mind. I was determined to persevere. I went up to one of the chiefs, made him understand that I had great news for Captain FitzGibbon, and that he must let me pass to his camp, or that he and his party would all be taken. The chief at first objected to let me pass, but finally consented, after some hesitation, to go with me and accompany me to FitzGibbon's station, which was at the Beaver Dam, where I had an interview with him. I then told him what I had come for and what I had heard—that the Americans intended to make an attack upon the troops under his command and would, from their superior numbers, capture them all. Benefiting by this information, Captain FitzGibbon formed his plans accordingly, and captured about five hundred American infantry, about fifty mounted dragoons ; and a field piece or two was taken from the enemy. I returned home the next day exhausted and fatigued. I am now advanced in years, and when I look back I wonder how I could have gone through so much fatigue with the fortitude to accomplish it.

27. THE BATTLE OF LUNDY'S LANE, 25 JULY, 1814.

Source.—*The Annual Register* for 1814.

After the action near Chippawa, General Riall retreated to a position near Fort Niagara, and the American army took post at Chippawa. The British force in Canada had been at this time augmented by the arrival at Quebec of some transports from Bordeaux, conveying veteran troops which had served under Lord Wellington in Spain. On July 25th, General Drummond, arriving at Niagara, found that General Riall had moved forward to the Falls in order to support the advance of his division at that place ; and he despatched Lieut.-Col. Morrison with the 39th regiment and detachments of two others, in order that he might, if necessary, act with the united force of the army, against the enemy posted at Street's creek, with his advance at Chippawa. General Drummond, proceeding to join General Riall, learned that the Americans were advancing in great force; and, pushing forwards, he found that the advance of Riall's division had commenced their retreat. He immediately drew up his troops in line of battle, when his whole front was warmly and closely engaged. The Americans gained a temporary advantage, during which General Riall, having been severely wounded, was made prisoner. In the centre, the enemy's repeated and determined attacks were resisted with the greatest steadiness and intrepidity by the detachments of the Royals and King's and the light company of the 41st ; and so obstinate was the encounter that the British artillerymen were bayoneted while in the act of loading, and the muzzles of the enemy's guns were brought within a few yards of those of their opponents. The action continued from six in the evening to nine, when there was a short intermission, during which the Americans were employed in bringing up the whole of their remaining force, and with this they renewed their efforts to carry the height on which the British were posted till about midnight. The gallantry with which they were received and their severe losses at length obliged them to give up the contest, and retreat with precipitation beyond the Chippawa. On the following day they abandoned their camp, threw the greatest part of their baggage and provisions into the Rapids, and, having set fire to Street's mills and destroyed the bridge over the Chippawa, continued their retreat in great disorder to Fort Erie. General Drummond estimates the enemy's loss at not less than 1500, including several hundred prisoners ; their whole force, rated at 5000, having been engaged. The British force during the first three hours of the action did not exceed 1600 men, and the additional troops under Colonel Scott did not augment it beyond 2800 of all descriptions. Of these, the loss amounted in killed, wounded and missing to 878. In this manner was defeated another attempt of the Americans to penetrate into Canada ; respecting which, it cannot escape observation that, although British valour and discipline were finally triumphant, the improvement of the American troops in these qualities was eminently conspicuous.

28. THE ATTACK ON THE RED RIVER SETTLEMENT (1816).

Source.—A Narrative by Mr. Pritchard, one of the principal settlers, quoted in a *Statement respecting the Earl of Selkirk's Settlement upon the Red River*, published by the personal friends of the Earl in London in 1817.

In the course of the winter we were much alarmed by reports that the Half-breeds were assembling in all parts of the North for the purpose of driving us away, and that they were expected to arrive at the settlement early in the spring. The nearer the spring approached, the more prevalent these reports grew, and letters received from different posts confirmed the same. Our hunters and those free Canadians who had supplied us with provisions were much terrified with the dread of the punishment they might receive for the support they had given us. My neighbours, the Half-breeds, began to show a disposition to violence, and threatened to shoot our hunter Bollenaud's horse and himself too, if he did not desist from running the buffalo ; at the same time they told me that, if I did not prevent him from so doing, they would go in a body on horseback, drive the cattle away, and cause my people to starve.

In the month of March, Messrs. Fraser and Hesse arrived at my neighbour's house, which gave us great uneasiness, as Fraser was represented as the leader of the Half-breeds, and that he was a daring and violent man. On his arrival he sent a threatening message to one of my hunters ; and, whenever an opportunity offered, he was very assiduous in his endeavours to seduce from us our servants and settlers ; likewise a report was very current that a party of Half-breeds and Cree Indians were expected to arrive from Fort des Prairies on the Saskatchewan River, as soon as the melting of the snow would admit of their travelling ; and the language of every free Canadian we saw was " *Méfiez vous bien pour l'amour de Dieu ; méfiez vous bien.*" At the same time we were informed that the Half-breed servants of the North-West Company who were then in the plains, were ordered home to their house

The assemblage of those men gave us the most serious apprehensions for the safety of the settlers and those servants who were employed to bring provisions from the plains to the fort. . . .

On the afternoon of the 19th of June, a man in the watch-house called out that the Half-breeds were coming. The governor, some other gentlemen and myself, looked through spy-glasses, and I distinctly saw some armed people on horseback passing along the plains. A man then called out, "They (meaning the Half-breeds), are making for the settlers"; on which the governor said, "We must go out and meet these people; let twenty men follow me." We proceeded by the old road leading down the settlement. As we were going along, we met many of the settlers running to the fort, crying, "The Half-breeds, the Half-breeds." . . . We had not proceeded far, before the Half-breeds on horseback, with their faces painted in the most hideous manner and in the dresses of Indian warriors, came forward and surrounded us in the form of a half-moon. We then extended our line and moved more into the open plain; and, as they advanced, we retreated a few steps backwards, and then saw a Canadian named Boucher ride up to us waving his hand and calling out, "What do you want?" The governor replied, "What do you want?" To which Boucher answered, "We want our fort." The governor said, "Go to your fort." They were by this time near each other, and consequently spoke too low for me to hear. Being at some little distance to the right of the governor, I saw him take hold of Boucher's gun, and almost immediately a general discharge of fire-arms took place; but whether it began on our side or that of the enemy it was impossible to distinguish: my attention was then directed towards my personal defence. In a few minutes almost all our people were either killed or wounded. . . . I was rescued from death in the most providential manner no less than six different times on my road to, and at, the Frog Plain (the headquarters of those cruel murderers). . . . With the exception of myself, no quarter was given to any of us. . . . The amiable and mild Mr.

Semple, lying on his side (his thigh having been broken) and supporting his head upon his hand, addressed the chief commander of our enemies, by inquiring if he was Mr. Grant; and, being answered in the affirmative, " I am not mortally wounded," said Mr. Semple, " and, if you could get me conveyed to the fort, I think I should live." Grant promised he would do so; and immediately left him in the care of a Canadian, who afterwards told that an Indian of their party came up and shot Mr. Semple in the breast. I entreated Grant to procure me the watch or even the seals of Mr. Semple for the purpose of transmitting them to his friends, but I did not succeed. Our force amounted to twenty-eight persons, of whom twenty-one were killed and one wounded. . . . The enemy, I am told, were sixty-two persons, the greater part of whom were the contracted servants and clerks of the North-West Company. They had one man killed and one wounded.

29. PROPOSED UNION OF THE CANADAS (1822).

Source.—A Petition from the British Inhabitants of Montreal, December, 1822: printed in the *Report on the Canadian Archives for* 1897.

It is a consequence of the relative geographical situation of the Provinces, that Upper Canada is entirely dependent on Lower Canada for the means of communicating with the parent state and other countries; it is only through Lower Canada that the Upper Province can receive its supplies or export its surplus commodities.

The port of Quebec is the entrance common to both. This being situated in Lower Canada, the inhabitants of Upper Canada can have neither free ingress into, nor egress from, their country, except in so far as it may be permitted by the Government of Lower Canada. This, your Majesty's petitioners humbly represent, is a cause for the union of the Provinces perpetual in its operation, and which cannot be counteracted without a long series of inconveniences and disasters to both. If, while it may still be done, the population of the two Provinces be not gradually assimilated and identified in their interests by a union, the differences between them from the causes now in operation and the collisions to which they will give rise, must have the effect of rendering the inhabitants of each a separate and distinct people, with the most hostile feelings towards each other, requiring only a fit occasion to urge them into measures of actual violence. In the progress of things towards this conclusion, the inhabitants of Upper Canada would imperceptibly be induced to form connections with their American neighbours, and, being unnaturally disjoined from Lower Canada, would seek to diminish the inconveniences arising by a more intimate intercourse with the adjoining states, leading inevitably to a union with that country. The actual tendency of things to this result, while the Provinces continue under separate Legislatures, it is to be observed, is likely to be much promoted by the artificial means of communication by canals which have been lately formed at immense expense in the state of New York, affording to Upper Canada, if the outlet at the port of Quebec should be rendered inconvenient to her, an easy communication to American seaports; and her disposition to avail herself of this communication will obviously be increased while the Lower Province continues in its character to be French.

Some of the circumstances arising from the division of countries thus united by nature . . . have been practically exhibited in the disputes respecting revenue between the two Provinces. Upper Canada relies on the revenue to be derived from import duties for the payment of her civil expenditure. The nature of her local situation precludes her from conveniently or effectually levying these duties within her own limits; it is at the port of Quebec only that she can levy them: but this is in another Province, and, while she has a separate Legislature, beyond the authority of her Government. . . .

In adverting to the injurious consequences arising from the division of the late Province of Quebec, your Majesty's petitioners cannot omit to notice more particularly the effect that measure has had in preventing the increase of the British population in Lower Canada and the development of its resources. The preponderance of the French population in the Legislature has occasioned obstacles to the settlement of British emigrants that have not been surmounted ; so that the vast increase of British population to have been expected from this cause has been, in a general degree, prevented. The injury sustained in this particular may be easily appreciated when it is observed that, since the late American War, upwards of eighty thousand souls (that is, a number equal to one-fourth of the actual French population) have found their way to this Province from Great Britain and Ireland, and of these scarcely one-twentieth part remains within its limits, the rest, with the exception of a small number who have settled in Upper Canada, having been induced by the foreign character of the country in which they had sought an asylum, and the discouragements they experienced, to try their fortunes in the United States. The loss thus sustained is not confined to those who left the country, but comprises their connections and friends who would have followed them. In the same proportion as the increase of British population has been prevented, has the agricultural and commercial prosperity of the country been retarded and obstructed ; as it is to the enterprise, intelligence and persevering industry of that population that both agriculture and commerce must be principally indebted for their advancement. On this head it may be fairly advanced that, had not the impolitic division of the late Province of Quebec taken place, and had a fit plan of representation been adopted, the British population would now exceed the French, and the imports and exports of the country be greatly beyond their present amount.

30. THE FOUNDING OF GUELPH, ONTARIO (1827).

Source.—*The Autobiography of John Galt.* London, 1833.

On the 22nd of April, the day previous to the time appointed for laying the foundations of my projected polis, I went to Galt, a town situated on the banks of the Grand River, which my friend, the Honourable William Dixon, in whose township it is situated, named after me long before the Canada Company was imagined; it was arrived at the maturity of having a post office before I heard of its existence. There I met by appointment, at Mr. Dickson's, Dr. Dunlop, who held a roving commission in the Canada Company, and was informed that the requisite woodmen were assembled.

Next morning we walked after breakfast towards the site which had been selected. The distance was about eighteen miles from Galt, half of it in the forest, but till we came near the end of the road no accident happened. Scarcely, however, had we entered the bush, as the woods are called, when the doctor found he had lost the way. I was excessively angry, for such an accident is no trifle in the woods; but after " wandering up and down " like the two babes, with not even the comfort of a blackberry, the heavens frowning and the surrounding forest sullenly still, we discovered a hut, and " tirling at the pin " entered and found it inhabited by a Dutch shoemaker. We made him understand our lost condition, and induced him to set us on the right path. He had been in the French army, and had after the peace emigrated to the United States; thence he had come into Upper Canada, where he bought a lot of land, which, after he had made some betterments, he exchanged for the location in the woods, or as he said himself "Je swapé" the first land for the lot on which he was now settled.

With his assistance we reached the skirts of the wild to which we were going, and were informed in the cabin of a squatter that all our men had gone forward. By this time it began to rain, but undeterred by that circumstance we resumed our journey in the pathless wood. About sunset, dripping wet, we arrived near the spot we were in quest of, a shanty which an Indian who had committed murder had raised as a refuge for himself. . . .

We found the men under the orders of Mr. Prior, whom I had employed for the Company, kindling a roaring fire, and after endeavouring to dry ourselves, and having recourse to the store-basket, I proposed to go to the spot chosen for the town. By this time the sun was set, and Dr. Dunlop with his characteristic drollery having doffed his wet garb and dressed himself Indian fashion in blankets, we proceeded with Mr. Prior, attended by two woodmen with their axes.

It was consistent with my plan to invest our ceremony with a little mystery, the better to make it be remembered. So, intimating that the main body of the men were not to come, we walked to the brow of the neighbouring rising ground, and, Mr. Prior having shown the site selected for the town, a large maple tree was chosen, on which, taking an axe from one of the woodmen, I struck the first stroke. To me at least the moment was impressive—and the silence of the woods that echoed to the sound was as the sigh of the solemn genius of the wilderness departing for ever.

The doctor followed me ; then, if I recollect correctly, Mr. Prior, and the woodmen finished the work. The tree fell with a crash of accumulating thunder, as if ancient Nature were alarmed at the entrance of social man into her innocent solitudes with his sorrows, his follies, and his crimes.

I do not suppose that the sublimity of the occasion was unfelt by the others, for I noticed that after the tree fell there was a funereal pause, as when the coffin is lowered into the grave ; it was, however, of short duration, for the doctor pulled a flask of whiskey from his bosom, and we drank prosperity to the City of Guelph.

The name was chosen in compliment to the royal family, both because I thought it auspicious in itself, and because I could not recollect that it had ever been before used in all the King's dominions.

After the solemnity—for, though the ceremony was simple, it may be so denominated—we returned to the shanty, and the rain, which had been suspended during the performance, began again to pour.

It may appear ludicrous to many readers that I look on this incident with gravity, but in truth I am very serious ; for, although Guelph is not so situated as ever to become celebrated for foreign commerce, the location possesses many advantages independent of being situated on a tongue of land surrounded by a clear and rapid stream.   It will be seen by the map of the province that it stands almost in the centre of the table-land which separates four of the great lakes, namely, Ontario, Simcoe, Huron and Erie.

31. SAM SLICK CRITICISES THE " BLUENOSES " OR NOVA SCOTIANS (1836).

Source.—*The Clockmaker, or the Sayings and Doings of Samuel Slick*, by T. C. Haliburton.   London, 1838.

As we approached within fifteen or twenty miles of Parrs-boro', a sudden turn of the road brought us directly in front of a large wooden house, consisting of two stories and an immense roof, the height of which edifice was much increased by a stone foundation rising several feet above ground.   Now did you ever see, said Mr. Slick, such a catamaran as that ; there's a proper goney for you, for to go and raise such a building as that are ; and he has as much use for it, I do suppose, as my old waggon here has for a fifth wheel.   Blue-nose always takes keer to have a big house, cause it shows a big man, and one that's considerable forehanded, and pretty well to do in the world.   These Nova Scotians turn up their blue noses, as a bottle nose porpoise turns up his snout, and puff and snort exactly like him at a small house.   If neighbour Carrit has a two storey house, all filled with winders like Sandy Hook lighthouse, neighbour Parsnip must add jist two feet more on to the post of hisn, and about as much more to the rafter, to go ahead of him ; so all these long sarce gentle-

men strive who can get the furdest in the sky, away from their
farms. In New England our maxim is a small house and amost
an everlastin almighty big barn ; but these critters revarse ı
it, they have little hovels for their cattle, about the bigness of
a good sizeable bear trap, and a house for the humans as grand
as Noah's Ark. Well, jist look at it and see what a figur it does
cut. An old hat stuffed into one pane of glass, and an old
flannel petticoat as yaller as jaundice in another, finish off the
front ; an old pair of breeches and the pad of a bran new
cart-saddle worn out titivate the eend, while the back is all
closed up on account of the wind. When it rains, if there aint
a pretty how-do-you-do, it's a pity—beds toted out of this
room, and tubs set in tother to catch soft water to wash ;
while the clapboards, loose at the eends, go clap, clap, clap,
like gals a hacklin flax, and the winders and doors keep a
dancin to the music. The only dry place in the house is in
the chimbley corner, where the folks all huddle up, as an old
hen and her chickens do under a cart of a wet day. I wish I ı
had the matter of half a dozen pound of nails (you'll hear the
old gentleman in the grand house say), for if I had, I'd fix them
are clapboards ; I guess they'll go for it some o' these days.
I wish you had, his wife would say, for they do make a most
particular unhansum clatter, that's a fact ; and so they let it
be till the next tempestical time comes, and then they wish
agin. Now this grand house has only two rooms down stairs,
that are altogether slicked up and finished off complete ; the
other is jist petitioned off roughlike, one half great dark entries,
and tother half places that look a plaguy sight more like
packin' boxes than rooms. Well, all upstairs is a great on-
farnished place, filled with every sort of good for nothin
trumpery in natur—barrels without eends, corncobs half
husked, cast-off clothes and bits of old harness, sheep skins,
hides and wool, apples, one half rotten and tother half squashed,
a thousand or two of shingles that have bust their withs and
broke loose all over the floor, hay rakes, forks and sickles without handles or teeth, rusty scythes and odds and eends without
number. . . .

C.   E

Whenever you come to such a grand place as this Squire, depend on't the farm is all of a piece, great crops of thistles, and an everlastin yield of weeds, and cattle the best fed of any in the country, for they are always in the grain fields or mowin lands, and the pigs a rootin in the potatoe patches. . . .

The last time I came by here, it was a little bit arter daylight down, rainin cats and dogs and as dark as Egypt ; so, thinks I, I'll jist turn in here for shelter to Squire Bill Blake's. Well, I knocks away at the front door, till I thought I'd a split it in ; but arter a rappin a while to no purpose and findin no one come, I gropes my way round to the back door, and opens it, and feelin all along the partition for the latch of the keepin room without finding it, I knocks agin, when someone from inside calls out " Walk." Thinks I, I don't cleverly know whether that indicates " walk in " or " walk out," it's plaguy short metre, that's a fact ; but I'll see anyhow. Well, arter gropin about a while, at last I got hold of the string and lifted the latch and walked in, and there sot old Marm Blake, close into one corner of the chimbley fire-place, a see-sawin in a rockin-chair, and a half-grown black house-help, half asleep in tother corner, a scroudgin up over the embers. Who be you, said Marm Blake, for I can't see you. A stranger, said I. Beck, says she . . . get up this minit and stir the coals till I see the man. Arter the coals were stirred into a blaze, the old lady surveyed me from head to foot, then she axed me my name, and where I came from, where I was agoin, and what my business was. I guess, said she, you must be reasonable wet, sit to the fire and dry yourself, or mayhap your health may be endamnified pr'aps.

So I sot down, and we soon got pretty considerably well acquainted, and quite sociable like, and her tongue, when it fairly waked up, began to run like a mill race when the gate's up. . . . Well, when all was sot to rights and the fire made up, the old lady began to apologise for having no candles ; she said she'd had a grand tea party the night afore, and used them all up, and a whole sight of vittals too ; the old man hadn't been well since, and had gone to bed airly. But, says she, I do wish with all my heart you had a come last night, for we had a most a special supper—punkin-pies and dough-nuts and apple-sarce, and a roast goose stuffed with Indian puddin, and a pig's harslet stewed in molasses and onions, and I don't know what all ; and the fore part of to-day folks called to finish. I actilly have nothin left to set afore you ; for it was none o' your skim-milk parties, but superfine uppercrust real jam, and we made clean work of it. But I'll make some tea anyhow for you, and perhaps after that, said she, alterin of her tone, perhaps you'll expound the Scriptures, for it's one while since I've heerd them laid open powerfully. . . . The tea-kettle was accordingly put on, and some lard fried into oil and poured into a tumbler ; which, with the aid of an inch of cotton-wick, served as a makeshift for a candle.

32. A STRUGGLE, NOT OF PRINCIPLES, BUT OF RACES (1838).

Source.—Lord Durham's *Report on the Affairs of North America*, edited by Sir C. P. Lucas. Vol. II. Oxford, 1912.

From the peculiar circumstances in which I was placed, I was enabled to make such effectual observations as convinced me that there had existed in the constitution of the Province, in the balance of political powers, in the spirit and practice of administration in every department of the Government, defects that were quite sufficient to account for a great deal of mismanagement and dissatisfaction. The same observation had also impressed on me the conviction, that, for the peculiar and disastrous dissensions of this Province, there existed a far deeper and far more efficient cause,—a cause which penetrated beneath its political institutions into its social state,—a cause which no reform of constitution or laws, that should leave the elements of society unaltered, could remove ; but which must be removed, ere any success could be expected in any attempt to remedy the many evils of this unhappy Province. I expected to find a contest between a government and a people : I found two nations warring in the bosom of a single state : I found a

struggle, not of principles, but of races, and I perceived that it
would be idle to attempt any amelioration of laws or institutions until we could first succeed in terminating the deadly
animosity that now separates the inhabitants of Lower Canada
into the hostile divisions of French and English. . . .

The grounds of quarrel which are commonly alleged, appear,
on investigation, to have little to do with its real cause ; and
the inquirer, who has imagined that the public demonstrations
or professions of the parties have put him in possession of their
real motives and designs, is surprised to find, upon nearer
observation, how much he has been deceived by the false
colours under which they have been in the habit of fighting.
It is not, indeed, surprising, that each party should, in this
instance, have practised more than the usual frauds of
language, by which factions, in every country, seek to secure
the sympathy of other communities. A quarrel based on the
mere ground of national animosity, appears so revolting to
the notions of good sense and charity prevalent in the civilised
world, that the parties who feel such a passion the most
strongly, and indulge it the most openly, are at great pains to
class themselves under any denominations but those which
would correctly designate their objects and feelings. The
French Canadians have attempted to shroud their hostility
to the influence of English emigration, and the introduction
of British institutions, under the guise of warfare against the
Government and its supporters, whom they represented to be
a small knot of corrupt and insolent dependents ; being a
majority, they have invoked the principles of popular control
and democracy, and appealed with no little effect to the sympathy of liberal politicians in every quarter of the world. The
English, finding their opponents in collision with the Government, have raised the cry of loyalty and attachment to British
connexion, and denounced the republican designs of the
French, whom they designate by the appellation of Radicals.
Thus the French have been viewed as a democratic party, con-
tending for reform ; and the English as a conservative minority, protecting the menaced connexion with the British Crown,

and the supreme authority of the Empire. There is truth in this notion in so far as respects the means by which each party sought to carry its own views of Government into effect. The French majority asserted the most democratic doctrines of the rights of a numerical majority. The English minority availed itself of the protection of the prerogative, and allied itself with all those of the colonial institutions which enabled the few to resist the will of the many. But when we look to the objects of each party, the analogy to our own politics seems to be lost if not actually reversed ; the French appear to have used their democratic arms for conservative purposes, rather than those of liberal and enlightened movement ; and the sympathies of the friends of reform are naturally enlisted on the side of sound amelioration which the English minority in vain attempted to introduce into the antiquated laws of the Province.

33. THE FRENCH CANADIANS IN 1838.

Source.—Appendix ' C " to Lord Durham's *Report*. Lucas. Vol. III.

The *habitants*, or agricultural population of French origin, hold their lands by feudal tenure, which prevails in the " seignorial " districts. Though under the sway of England for 75 years, they are but little changed in usages, and not at all in language. A very small proportion of them are acquainted with the first rudiments of education ; they use comparatively few imported articles, and their system of agriculture is generally rude and antiquated. Owing to the neglect of manure and a proper rotation of crops, the land in many places has become exhausted, and its cultivators, year after year, sink deeper in poverty. Scanty harvests during the last six or eight years, caused mainly by imperfect modes of culture or injudicious cropping, have reduced considerable numbers of the *habitants* in the district of Quebec to a state of extreme destitution. In the district of Montreal, the farming is better, and the people more prosperous. The *habitant* is active, hardy and intelligent, but excitable, credulous ; and, being a stranger to everything beyond his own contracted sphere, he is peculiarly liable to be made the dupe of political speculators. His ignorance of the English language prevents him from acquiring any knowledge of the sentiments and views of the British Government and people, except what he may derive from educated persons of his own race, interested, it may be, in deceiving him. Never having *directly* experienced the benefits of British rule in local affairs, and almost as much insulated from British social influences as if the colony had never changed masters, it is idle to expect that he should entertain any active feeling of attachment to the Crown.

For opening new settlements the *habitant* has many useful qualifications, being usually competent to provide, by his personal skill, all the essentials requisite for his situation, such as house, clothing, and the ordinary farming implements. But having cleared his land, erected a dwelling for himself and a church for the *curé*, he remains stationary, contented with his lot, and living and dying as his ancestors lived and died before him. At the present day, for instance, a traveller may pass through districts where there is an abundance of excellent milk, and be unable to procure either butter or cheese with the sour and black-looking country bread which is served up at his meals ; and it is by no means an uncommon circumstance for a *habitant* to sell his manure to a neighbouring farmer, or throw it into the adjoining river, while every season his crops are deteriorating, in consequence of the degeneracy of the seed and the exhaustion of the soil.

By the *habitant* a small gain, or saving of actual coin, is deemed much more important than a large expenditure of time ; and he will not easily be induced to venture on an immediate pecuniary outlay to secure a remote advantage, unless indeed the money is to be devoted to litigation, in which he loves to indulge.

There is no class resembling English " country gentlemen " among the Canadians ; nor do the doctors, notaries and lawyers, who overabound in the colony, form an efficient substitute for such a class. Needy and discontented, they are more disposed to attempt an improvement in their own condition of political agitation, than to labour for the advancement of their uninstructed neighbours. The only body of men to whom the *habitants* can look for aid and direction are the parochial clergy, who, in the districts where their authority is unimpaired, act as a vigilant moral police, the efficiency of which is manifested in established habits of sobriety and order. Persons acquainted with the province are well aware that, in the disaffected districts, the influence of the Canadian clergy is much diminished.

It appears, then, that the mode of village settlement adopted by the Franco-Canadians is favourable to the establishment of municipal institutions, and that the obstacles to be encountered are the absence of education, popular inexperience, blind repugnance to taxation, and the absence of a wealthy and instructed class, interested in the prosperity of the many, and desirous of engaging gratuitously in the administration of local affairs.

34. THE IRRESPONSIBLE OPPOSITION IN LOWER CANADA (1838).

Source.—Lord Durham's *Report.* Lucas. Vol. II.

It appears, therefore, that the opposition of the Assembly to the Government was the unavoidable result of a system which stinted the popular branch of the legislature of the necessary privileges of a representative body, and produced thereby a long series of attempts on the part of that body to acquire control over the administration of the Province. I say all this without reference to the ultimate aim of the Assembly, which I have before described as being the maintenance of a Canadian nationality against the progressive intrusion of the English race. Having no responsible ministers to deal with, it entered upon that system of long inquiries by means of its committees, which brought the whole action of the executive immediately under its purview, and transgressed our notions of the proper limits of Parliamentary interference. Having no influence in the choice of any public functionary, no power to procure the removal of such as were obnoxious to it merely on political grounds, and seeing almost every office of the Colony filled by persons in whom it had no confidence, it entered on that vicious course of assailing its prominent opponents individually, and disqualifying them for the public service, by making them the subjects of inquiries and consequent impeachments, not always conducted with even the appearance of a due regard to justice ; and when nothing else could attain its end of altering the policy or the composition of the colonial government, it had recourse to that *ultima ratio* of representative power to which the more prudent forbearance of the Crown has never driven the House of Commons in England, and endeavoured to disable the whole machine of Government by a general refusal of the supplies.

It was an unhappy consequence of the system which I have been describing, that it relieved the popular leaders of all the responsibilities of opposition. A member of opposition in this country acts and speaks with the contingency of becoming a minister constantly before his eyes, and he feels, therefore, the necessity of proposing no course, and of asserting no principles, on which he would not be prepared to conduct the Government, if he were immediately offered it. But the colonial demagogue bids high for popularity without the fear of future exposure. Hopelessly excluded from power, he expresses the wildest opinion, and appeals to the most mischievous passions of the people, without any apprehension of having his sincerity or prudence hereafter tested, by being placed in a position to carry his views into effect ; and thus the prominent places in the ranks of opposition are occupied for the most part by men of strong passions, and merely declamatory powers, who think but little of reforming the abuses which serve them as topics for exciting discontent.

35. DURHAM'S RECOMMENDATIONS (1838).

Source.—Lord Durham's *Report*. Lucas. Vol. II.

It is not by weakening, but strengthening the influence of the people on its Government ; by confining within much narrower bounds than those hitherto allotted to it, and not by extending the interference of the imperial authorities in the details of colonial affairs; that I believe that harmony is to be restored, where dissension has so long prevailed, and a regularity and vigour hitherto unknown, introduced into the administration of these Provinces. It needs no change in the principles of government, no invention of a new constitutional theory, to supply the remedy which would, in my opinion, completely remove the existing political disorders. It needs but to follow out consistently the principles of the British constitution, and introduce into the Government of these great Colonies those wise provisions, by which alone the working of the representative system can in any country be rendered harmonious and efficient. We are not now to consider the policy of establishing representative government in the North American Colonies. That has been irrevocably done ; and the experiment of depriving the people of their present constitutional power, is not to be thought of. To conduct their government harmoniously, in accordance with its established principles, is now the business of its rulers ; and I know not how it is possible to secure that harmony in any other way than by administering the Government on those principles which have been found perfectly efficacious in Great Britain. I would not impair a single prerogative of the Crown ; on the contrary, I believe that the interests of the people of these colonies require the protection of prerogatives, which have not hitherto been exercised. But the Crown must, on the other hand, submit to the necessary consequences of representative institutions ; and, if it has to carry on the Government in unison with a representative body, it must consent to carry it on by means of those in whom that representative body has confidence. . . .

These general principles apply, however, only to those changes in the system of government which are required in order to rectify disorders common to all the North American Colonies ; but they do not in any degree go to remove those evils in the present state of Lower Canada which require the most immediate remedy. The fatal feud of origin, which is the cause of the most extensive mischief, would be aggravated at the present moment by any change, which should give the majority more power than they have hitherto possessed. A plan by which it is proposed to ensure the tranquil government of Lower Canada, must include in itself the means of putting an end to the agitation of national disputes in the legislature, by settling, at once and for ever, the national character of the Province. I entertain no doubts as to the national character which must be given to Lower Canada ; it must be that of the British Empire ; that of the majority of the population of British America ; that of the great race which must, in the lapse of no long period of time, be predominant over the whole North American Continent. Without effecting the change so rapidly or so roughly as to shock the feelings and trample on the welfare of the existing generation, it must henceforth be the first and steady purpose of the British Government to establish an English population, with English laws and language, in this Province, and to trust its government to none but a decidedly English legislature. . . .

It is only . . . by a popular government, in which an English majority shall permanently predominate, that Lower Canada, if a remedy for its disorders be not too long delayed, can be tranquilly ruled.

On these grounds, I believe that no permanent or efficient remedy can be devised for the disorders of Lower Canada, except a fusion of the Government in that of one or more of the surrounding Provinces ; and, as I am of opinion that the full establishment of responsible government can only be permanently secured by giving these Colonies an increased importance in the politics of the Empire, I find in union the only means of remedying at once and completely the two prominent causes of their present unsatisfactory condition.

36. DURHAM RESIGNS AND APPEALS TO PUBLIC OPINION (1838).

Source.—Durham's Proclamation of 9th October, 1838, quoted in *The Report and Despatches of the Earl of Durham*. London, 1839.

. . . I have also to notify the disallowance by her Majesty of the Ordinance . . . " to provide for the security of the Province of Lower Canada."

I cannot perform these official duties without at the same time informing you, the people of British America, of the course which the measures of the Imperial Government and Legislature make it incumbent on me to pursue. . . .

I did not accept the Government of British North America without duly considering the nature of the task which I imposed on myself, or the sufficiency of my means for performing it. When Parliament concentrated all legislative and executive power in Lower Canada in the same hands, it established an authority, which, in the strictest sense of the word, was despotic. This authority her Majesty was graciously pleased to delegate to me. . . .

To encourage and stimulate me in my arduous task, I had great and worthy objects in view. My aim was to elevate the province of Lower Canada to a thoroughly British character, to link its people to the sovereignty of Britain, by making them all participators in those high privileges, conducive at once to freedom and order, which have long been the glory of Englishmen. I hoped to confer on an united people, a more extensive enjoyment of free and responsible government, and to merge the petty jealousies of a small community, and the odious animosities of origin, in the higher feelings of a nobler and more comprehensive nationality. . . .

I had reason to believe that I was armed with all the power which I thought requisite. . . . I also trusted that I should enjoy, throughout the course of my administration, all the strength which the cordial and steadfast support of the authorities at home can alone give to their distant officers ; and that even party feeling would refrain from molesting me whilst occupied in maintaining the integrity of the British Empire.

In these just expectations I have been painfully disappointed. From the very commencement of my task, the minutest details of my administration have been exposed to incessant criticism, in a spirit which has evinced an entire ignorance of the state of this country, and of the only mode in which the supremacy of the British Crown can here be upheld and exercised. Those who have in the British Legislature systematically depreciated my powers, and the ministers of the Crown by their tacit acquiescence therein, have produced the effect of making it too clear that my authority is inadequate for the emergency which called it into existence. At length an act of my Government, the first and most important which was brought under the notice of the authorities at home, has been annulled ; and the entire policy, of which that act was a small though essential part, has thus been defeated. . . .

In these conflicting and painful circumstances, it is far better that I should at once and distinctly announce my intention of desisting from the vain attempt to carry my policy and system of administration into effect with such inadequate and restricted means. . . .

You will easily believe that, after all the exertions which I have made, it is with feelings of deep disappointment that I find myself thus suddenly deprived of the power of conferring great benefit on that province to which I have referred ; of reforming the administrative system there, and eradicating the manifold abuses which had been engendered by the negligence and corruption of former times, and so lamentably fostered by civil dissensions. I cannot but regret being obliged to renounce the still more glorious hope of employing unusual legislative powers in the endowment of that province with those free municipal institutions, which are the only sure basis of local improvement and representative liberty, of establishing a system of general education, of revising the defective laws which regulate real property and commerce, and of introducing a pure and competent administration of justice. Above all, I grieve to be thus forced to abandon the realisation of such large and solid schemes of colonisation and internal improvement, as would connect the distant portions of these extensive colonies, and lay open the unwrought treasures of the wilderness to the wants of British industry and the energy of British enterprise.

. . . Our exertions, however, will not, cannot be thrown away. The information which we have acquired, although not as yet fit for the purposes of immediate legislation, will contribute to the creation of juster views as to the resources, the wants and the interests of these colonies, than ever yet prevailed in the mother country.

37. THE EVILS OF THE OLD COLONIAL SYSTEM (1839).[1]

Source.—The open letters of Joseph Howe of Nova Scotia to the Colonial Secretary, Lord John Russell, 1839, printed in Howe's *Speeches and Public Letters*, Vol. II. Boston, 1858.

The city of Liverpool shall again serve us for the purposes of illustration. Turn back to the passages where I have described a Mayor, ignorant of everything, surrounded by irresponsible but cunning advisers ; who, for their own advantage, embroil him with a majority of the citizens, while his countenance, and the patronage created by the taxes levied upon the city, are monopolised by a miserable minority of the whole ; and insulted and injured thousands, swelling with indignation, surround him on every side. After your Lordship has dwelt upon this scene of heartburning and discontent—of general dissatisfaction among the citizens—of miserable intrigue and chuckling triumph, indulged by the few who squander the resources and decide on the interests of the many, but laugh at their murmurs and never acknowledge their authority—let me beg of you to

[1] Representative institutions without responsible government.

reflect whether matters would be made better or worse, if the Mayor of Liverpool was bound, in every important act of his administration, to ask the direction of, and throw the responsibility on, another individual, who never saw the city, who knows less about it than even himself, and who resides, not in London, at the distance of a day's coaching from him, but across the Atlantic, in Halifax, Quebec or Toronto, and with whom it is impossible to communicate about anything within a less period than a couple of months. Suppose that this gentleman in the distance possesses a veto upon every important ordinance by which the city is to be watched, lighted and improved—by which docks are to be formed, trade regulated, and one-third of the city revenues (drawn from sources beyond the control of the popular branch) dispensed. And suppose that nearly all whose talents or ambition lead them to aspire to the higher offices of the place, are compelled to take, once or twice in their lives, a voyage across the Atlantic, to pay their court to him— to solicit his patronage, and intrigue for the preferment, which, under a better system, would naturally result from manly competition and eminent services within the city itself. Your Lordship is too keen sighted, and I trust too frank, not to acknowledge that no form of government could well be devised more ridiculous than this ; that under such no British city could be expected to prosper ; and that with it no body of her Majesty's subjects, within the British islands themselves, would ever be content. Yet this, my Lord, is an illustration of your own theory ; this is the system propounded by Lord Normanby,[1] as the best the present cabinet can devise. And may I not respectfully demand, why British subjects in Nova Scotia any more than their brethren in Liverpool, should be expected to prosper or be contented under it ; when experience has convinced them that it is miserably insufficient and deceptive, repugnant to the principles of the Constitution they revere, and but a poor return for the steady loyalty which their forefathers and themselves have maintained on all occasions ?

[1] Colonial Secretary in the early part of 1839.

One of the greatest evils of the Colonial Constitution, as interpreted by Your Lordship, is, that it removes from a Province every description of responsibility, and leaves all the higher functionaries at liberty to lay every kind of blame at the door of the Secretary of State. The Governor, if the Colonists complain, shrugs his shoulders, and replies that he will explain the difficulty in his next despatch, but in the meantime his orders must be obeyed.

38. THE BENEFITS OF RESPONSIBLE GOVERNMENT (1839).

Source—Howe's *Letters*, as in 37.

You ask me for the remedy. Lord Durham has stated it distinctly : the Colonial Governors must be commanded to govern by the aid of those who possess the confidence of the people, and are supported by a majority of the representative branch. Where is the danger ? Of what consequence is it to the people of England, whether half a dozen persons, in whom that majority have confidence, but of whom they know nothing and care less, manage our local affairs ; or the same number, selected from the minority, and whose policy the bulk of the population distrust ? . . . Would England be weaker, less prosperous or less respected, because the people of Nova Scotia were satisfied and happy ?

But, it is said, a Colony, being part of a great Empire, must be governed by different principles from the Metropolitan State. That, unless it be handed over to the minority, it cannot be governed at all. That the majority, when they have things their own way, will be discontented and disloyal. . . . Let us fancy that this reasoning were applied to Glasgow or Aberdeen or to any other town in Britain which you allow to govern itself. And what else is a Province like Nova Scotia than a small community, too feeble to interfere with the general commercial and military arrangements of the government ; but deeply interested in a number of minor matters, which only the people to be affected by them can wisely manage ; which the ministry can never find leisure to attend to, and involve in inextricable confusion when they meddle with them. You allow a million of people to govern themselves in the very capital of the kingdom ; and yet her Majesty lives in the midst of them without any apprehension of danger, and feels the more secure, the more satisfaction and tranquillity they exhibit. Of course, if the Lord Mayor were to declare war upon France, or the Board of Aldermen were to resolve that the duties upon brandy should no longer be collected by the general revenue officers of the kingdom, everybody would laugh, but no one would apprehend any great danger. Should we, if Lord Durham's principles be adopted, do anything equally *outré*, check us, for you have the power ; but until we do, for your own sakes—for you are as much interested as we are,—for the honour of the British name, too often tarnished by these squabbles, let us manage our own affairs, pay our own officers, and distribute a patronage, altogether beneath your notice, among those who command our esteem.

39. THE UNION ACT (1840).

Source.—*Documents Illustrative of the Canadian Constitution*, edited by William Houston. Toronto, 1891.

Whereas it is necessary that provision be made for the good government of the provinces of Upper and Lower Canada, in such manner as may secure the rights and liberties and promote the interests of all classes of her Majesty's subjects within the same : And whereas to this end it is expedient that the said provinces be reunited to form one province for the purposes of executive government and legislation. . . .

III. . . . from and after the reunion of the said two provinces there shall be within the Province of Canada one Legislative Council and one Assembly. . . .

IV. . . . for the purpose of composing the Legislative Council . . . it shall be lawful for her Majesty . . . to authorise the Governor in her Majesty's name, by an instrument under the Great Seal of the said Province, to summon to the said Legislative Council . . . such persons, being not fewer than twenty, as her Majesty shall think fit. . . .

V. . . . every member of the Legislative Council . . . shall hold his seat therein for the term of his life. . . .

XII. . . . in the Legislative Assembly . . . the parts of the said Province which now constitute the provinces of Upper and Lower Canada respectively, shall . . . be represented by an equal number of representatives to be elected for the places and in the manner hereinafter mentioned. . . .

XXXI. . . . there shall be a session of the Legislative Council and Assembly . . . once at least in every year . . . every Legislative Assembly . . . shall continue for four years from the day of the return of the writs for choosing the same, and no longer, subject nevertheless to be sooner prorogued or dissolved by the Governor of the said Province.

(Compare with IV. the Amendment Act of 1854.)

It shall be lawful for the Legislature of Canada . . . to alter the manner of composing the Legislative Council . . . and to make it consist of such number of members appointed or to be appointed or elected by such persons and in such manner as to the said Legislature may seem fit. . . .

(In accordance with this enabling Act of Parliament, a Canadian Act for making the Council elective was passed in 1856.)

40. EDMONTON IN 1841.

Source.—*Narrative of a Journey round the World,* by Sir George Simpson, Governor-in-Chief of the Hudson Bay Company's Territories in North America. London, 1847.

Next morning, being the 22nd of July, we had a sharp frost before sunrise, and afterwards a heavy dew. The whole country was so parched up, that no water could be found for breakfast till eleven o'clock ; and again in the afternoon we passed over a perfectly arid plain of about twenty-five miles

in length, encamping for the night at the commencement of
the Chaine des Lacs, a succession of small lakes stretching
over a distance of twenty or thirty miles. During the afternoon we saw our first raspberries ; they proved to be of large
size and fine flavour. Two days previously we had feasted on
the service-berry . . . a sort of cross between the cranberry
and the black currant ; and, before leaving Red River, we had
found wild strawberries ripe. . . .

Next afternoon we passed over a space of about four miles
in length, where the grass was thoroughly beaten down,
apparently the work of hail. Such storms, which are almost
always partial in their operation, are often remarkably furious
in this country. While travelling from Red River to Canada
in the fall of 1837, I was overtaken near Lac la Pluie by a
violent tempest of the kind, which, if we had not gained the
fort in time, might have proved fatal. As the angular masses
of ice rattled on the roof, we entertained fears for the safety
ı of the building ; and, in point of fact, the lodges of the Indians
were thrown down and their canoes shattered ; while their
luckless dogs, tumbling about like drunken men, scrambled
away howling in quest of shelter. Some of the pieces . . . we
found to be fully five inches and a half in circumference.

Throughout this country everything is in extremes—un-
paralleled cold and excessive heat ; long droughts, balanced
by drenching rain and destructive hail. But it is not in climate
only that these contrarieties prevail ; at some seasons both
whites and natives are living, in wasteful abundance, on
venison, buffalo, fish, and game of all kinds ; while at other
times they are reduced to the last degree of hunger, often
passing several days without food.

In the year 1820, when wintering at Athabasca Lake, our
provisions fell short at the establishment, and on two or three
occasions I went for three whole days and nights without
having a single morsel to swallow ; but then again I was one
of a party of eleven men and one woman, which discussed
three ducks and twenty-two geese at a sitting. . . .

The nights were getting chilly ; and, whenever the sky was

clear, a heavy dew fell from sunset to sunrise on particular spots, so as to look, when morning dawned, like large lakes in the distance. As the power of the sun increased, these mists gradually resolved themselves into streaks of various shapes and sizes, which, rising from the ground in the form of clouds, finally disappeared. . . .

The whole plain was covered with a luxuriant crop of the vetch or wild pea, almost as nutritious a food for cattle and horses as oats. As we drew near to the Saskatchewan, we had to cross as many as five creeks with steep and lofty banks, the last in particular being a stream scarcely twenty feet in span between rugged declivities about two hundred feet in height. . . .

On arriving in front of Edmonton, which was on the opposite bank of the Saskatchewan, we notified our approach by a volley of musketry, which was returned by the cannon of the fort. . . .

Edmonton is a well-built place, something of a hexagon in form. It is surrounded by high pickets and bastions, which, with the battlemented gateways, the flagstaffs, etc., give it a good deal of a martial appearance ; and it occupies a commanding situation, crowning an almost perpendicular part of the bank, about two hundred feet in height. The river is nearly as wide as at Carlton, while the immediate banks are well wooded, and the country behind consists of rolling prairies.

This fort, both inside and outside, is decorated with paintings and devices to suit the tastes of the savages that frequent it. Over the gateways are a most fanciful variety of vanes ; but the hall, of which both the ceiling and the walls present the gaudiest colours and the most fantastic sculptures, absolutely rivets the astonished natives to the spot with wonder and admiration. The buildings are smeared with a red earth found in the neighbourhood, which, when mixed with oil, produces a durable brown.

The vicinity is rich in mineral productions. A seam of coal, about ten feet in depth, can be traced for a very considerable distance along both sides of the river . . .

41. THE MOHAWK INDIANS IN ONTARIO (1842).

Source—*Letters from America*, by John Robert Godley.   London, 1844.

Within two miles of Brantford (which is called after Brandt
the Indian chief) is a village which may be termed the headquarters of the Mohawk tribe of Indians.   They lost their
possessions in the States by adhering to Great Britain in the
revolutionary war, and received in compensation a settlement
here of 160,000 acres: since that time they have decreased
considerably, and now consist of not more than 2200 souls.
I went over to the Indian village on Sunday morning, and
attended Divine service in their church; it was performed
according to the forms of the English Church, but in the
Mohawk language, with the exception of the sermon, which the
clergyman delivered in English, and which was translated with
wonderful fluency, sentence after sentence, by an Indian inter-
preter who stood beside him.   It was good, practical, and well
adapted to the audience, who listened with the most unfailing
attention, though the plan of proceeding made it necessarily
very long: the Indian language, too, is far more prolix than
ours, at least the sentences as translated were at least three
times as long as in the original delivery; the singing was
particularly good in point of time and harmony, but the airs
were somewhat monotonous.   Two children were baptised
during the service, one of them ensconced in a bark cradle,
which fitted it accurately, and was attached in a curious manner
to a board so as to be carried easily upon the mother's back.
There were about 120 Indians present; the men, with one or
two exceptions, dressed like Europeans, but the women wearing
their native costume, which is rather becoming: it consists of
a calico or linen tunic reaching to the knee, below which appears
a petticoat of blue cloth, generally embroidered with red and
white bead-work, the legs are covered with a kind of buskin
of blue cloth, and the feet with mocassins; over all is a large
robe or mantle, of blue cloth also, thrown loosely round the
shoulders; completing a dress which, at this time of year,

must be dreadfully hot and heavy : the head is without any other covering except very thick black shining hair. Those of the men who have not adopted the European costume wear instead of trousers a tunic and leggings which reach half-way up the thigh.

I had some conversation with the clergyman after service : he is employed by the " New England Society," has been for a long time among the Indians, and knows them well : he has a better opinion of them and of their capacity for acquiring domestic and industrious habits, than most white men to whom I have spoken upon the subject have expressed. The society support a school in the village, where about forty children are boarded, educated, and instructed in trades ; and they learn, Mr. N. says, as fast as Europeans : as yet, however, they are not fit to be trusted in making bargains with the whites, nor can they at all compete in matters of business with them : much of their original grant has been trafficked away to settlers, at prices wholly inadequate ; and, though such transactions are altogether illegal, they have been overlooked so long that it is now impossible to annul them. A superintendent lives close to the village, who is paid by Government for the express purpose of protecting the Indian interests and managing their affairs ; yet encroachments upon their rights are still perpetually made, which, however advantageous they may appear to a political economist, are neither reconcilable with equity nor with the real wishes and intentions of Government. Mr. N. is by no means without hopes that in a generation or two these Indians may become quite civilised : they are giving up their wandering habits, and settling rapidly upon farms throughout their territory ; and, in consequence, probably, of this change in their mode of life, the decrease in their numbers, which threatened a complete extinction of the tribe, has ceased of late years : if it turn out as he expects, this will form the sole exception to the general law which affects their people. They are very much attached (as well they may be) to the British Government ; and in 1837 turned out under their chiefs to the number of 500, and offered their services to it : they wished to attack Navy Island in their canoes, but those who were in command thought the enterprise too hazardous. The chiefs (whose office is, as among the ancient Gothic nations, partly hereditary and partly elective, *i.e.* ordinarily transmitted from father to son, but liable to be transferred in cases of incapacity) have still a good deal of authority among them, but, as it is of course not recognised by law, they are gradually losing it ; in fact, the race is assimilating itself here far more than anywhere else to the habits and manners of the surrounding Europeans, while at the same time there is perhaps hardly any settlement where the red blood is preserved with less mixture.

42. THE POSITION OF THE GOVERNOR (1854).

Source.—Lord Elgin to the Colonial Secretary, Sir George Grey, 18th December, 1854 : Elgin's *Letters and Journals*. London, 1872.

As the Imperial Government and Parliament gradually withdraw from legislative interference, and from the exercise of patronage in Colonial affairs, the office of Governor tends to become, in the most emphatic sense of the term, the link which connects the Mother-country and the Colony, and his influence the means by which harmony of action between the local and imperial authorities is to be preserved. It is not, however, in my humble judgment, by evincing an anxious desire to stretch to the utmost constitutional principles in his favour, but, on the contrary, by the frank acceptance of the conditions of the Parliamentary system, that this influence can be most surely extended and confirmed. Placed by his position above the strife of parties—holding office by a tenure less precarious than the ministers who surround him—having no political interests to serve but that of the community whose affairs he is appointed to administer—his opinion cannot fail, when all cause for suspicion and jealousy is removed, to have great weight in the Colonial Councils, while he is set at liberty to constitute himself in an especial manner the patron of those larger and higher interests—such interests, for example, as those of education, and of moral and material progress in all its branches—which, unlike the contests of party, unite instead of dividing the members of the body politic.

43. THE CONFEDERATION DEBATES (1865).

(1) *For Confederation :* (a) *J. A. Macdonald.*

Source.—*Debates in the Parliament of Canada on the Confederation of British North America, 1865.*

The colonies are now in a transition state. Gradually a different colonial system is being developed—and it will become year by year less a case of dependence on our part, and of overruling protection on the part of the Mother-country, and more a case of a healthy and cordial alliance. Instead of looking upon us as a merely dependent colony, England will have in us a friendly nation—a subordinate but still a powerful people—to stand by her in North America in peace or in war. The people of Australia will be such another subordinate nation. And England will have this advantage, if her colonies progress under the new colonial system, as I believe they will, that, though at war with all the rest of the world, she will be able to look to the subordinate nations in alliance with her, and owning allegiance to the same sovereign, who will assist in enabling her again to meet the whole world in arms, as she has done before. And if, in the great Napoleonic war, with every port in Europe closed against her commerce, she was yet able to hold her own, how much more will that be the case when she has a colonial empire rapidly increasing in power, in wealth, in influence, and in position ? It is true that we stand in danger, as we have stood in danger again and again in Canada, of being plunged into war and suffering all its dreadful consequences, as the result of causes over which we have no control, by reason of this connection. This, however, did not intimidate us. At the very mention of the prospect of a war some time ago, how were the feelings of the people aroused from one extremity of British America to the other, and preparations made for meeting its worst consequences!

Although the people of this country are fully aware of the horrors of war—should a war arise, unfortunately, between the United States and England, and we all pray it never may —they are still ready to encounter all perils of that kind, for the sake of the connection with England. There is not one adverse voice, not one adverse opinion on that point. We all feel the advantages we derive from our connection with England. So long as that alliance is maintained, we enjoy, under her protection, the privileges of constitutional liberty according to the British system. We will enjoy here that which is the great test of constitutional freedom—we will have the rights of the minority respected. In all countries the rights of the majority take care of themselves, but it is only in countries like England, enjoying constitutional liberty, and safe from the tyranny of a single despot or of an unbridled democracy, that the rights of minorities are regarded. So long, too, as we form a portion of the British Empire, we shall have the example of her free institutions, of the high standard of the character of her statesmen and public men, of the purity of her legislation, and the upright administration of her laws. In this younger country one great advantage of our connection with Great Britain will be, that, under her auspices, inspired by her example, a portion of her empire, our public men will be actuated by principles similar to those which actuate the statesmen at home. These, although not material, physical benefits, of which you can make an arithmetical calculation, are of such overwhelming advantage to our future interests and standing as a nation, that to obtain them is well worthy of any sacrifices we may be called upon to make, and the people of this country are ready to make them.

44. For Confederation : (b) George Brown.

And well, Mr. Speaker, may the work we have unitedly proposed rouse the ambition and energy of every true man in British America. Look, sir, at the map of the Continent of America, and mark that island (Newfoundland) commanding the mouth of the noble river that almost cuts our Continent in twain. Well, sir, that island is equal in extent to the kingdom of Portugal. Cross the straits of the mainland, and you touch the hospitable shores of Nova Scotia, a country as large as the kingdom of Greece. Then mark the sister province of New Brunswick—equal in extent to Denmark and Switzerland combined. Pass up the river St. Lawrence to Lower Canada—a country as large as France. Pass on to Upper Canada—twenty thousand square miles larger than Great Britain and Ireland put together. Cross over the Continent to the shores of the Pacific, and you are in British Columbia, the land of golden promise,—equal in extent to the Austrian Empire. I speak not now of the vast Indian Territories that lie between—greater in extent than the whole soil of Russia— and that will ere long, I trust, be opened up to civilisation under the auspices of the British American Confederation. Well, sir, the bold scheme in your hands is nothing less than to gather all these countries into one—to organise them all under one government, with the protection of the British flag, and in heartiest sympathy and affection with our fellow-subjects in the land that gave us birth. Our scheme is to establish a government that will seek to turn the tide of European emigration into this northern half of the American Continent—that will strive to develop its great natural resources—and that will endeavour to maintain liberty, and justice, and Christianity throughout the land.

45. (2) *Against Confederation : Christopher Dunkin.*

We are going to be called upon to spend money for yet another kindred purpose, and a large amount too—and this, as a part of this scheme. Our star of empire is to wing its way westward ; and we are to confederate everything in its track, from Newfoundland to Vancouver's Island, this last included. But, between us and it, there lies the Hudson Bay territory. So, of course, we must acquire that for confederation purposes ; and the plan is, that before we get it we shall have to pay for the elephant—though, after we get him, we may find him costly and hard to keep. . . . .

Disguise it how you may, the idea that underlies this plan is this, and nothing else—that we are to create here a something—kingdom, viceroyalty or principality—something that will soon stand in the same position towards the British Crown that Scotland and Ireland stood in before they were legislatively united with England ; a something having no other tie to the Empire than the one tie of fealty to the British Crown —a tie which in the cases, first, of Scotland, and then of Ireland, was found, when the pinch came, to be no tie at all ; which did not restrain either Scotland or Ireland from courses so inconsistent with that of England as to have made it necessary that their relations should be radically changed, and a legislative union formed in place of a merely nominal union. Suppose you do create here a kingdom or a principality, bound to the Empire by this shadow of a tie, the day of trial cannot be far distant, when this common fealty will be found of as little use in our case as it was in theirs, when, in consequence, the question will force itself on the Empire and on us, between entire separation on the one hand, and a legislative union on the other. But a legislative union of British America with the United Kingdom must be, in the opinion of, one may say, everybody at home and here, a sheer utter impossibility ; and when the question shall come to be whether we are so to be merged in the United Kingdom or are to separate entirely from it, the answer can only be—"At whatever cost, we separate." Sir, I believe in my conscience that this step now proposed is one directly and inevitably tending to that other step ; and for that reason—even if I believed, as I do not, that it bid fair to answer ever so well in the other respects—because I am an Englishman and hold to the connection with England, I must be against this scheme. . . .

The real danger is not of war with the United States. It is from what I may call their pacific hostility—from trouble to be wrought by them within this country—trouble to arise out of refusal of reciprocity—repeal of the bonding system—

custom-house annoyances—passport annoyances ; from their fomenting difficulties here, and taking advantage of our local jealousies ; from the multiplied worries they may cause us by a judicious alternation of bullying and coaxing, the thousand incidents which may easily be made to happen if things are not going on quite well in this country, and the people and government of the States are minded to make us feel the consequences of our not getting on quite so well as we might. Whether the union of the States is restored or not, this kind of thing can go on. The danger is, that either the United States, or those portions of the United States which are near us, and which are really stronger than we are, and enterprising enough and ambitious enough, and not very fond of us, and not at all fond of the Mother-country, not at all unwilling to strike a blow at her and to make us subservient to their own interest and ambition—the danger is, I say, that the United States, or those portions of the United States near us, may avail themselves of every opportunity to perplex us, to embroil us in trouble, to make us come within the disturbing influences of their strong local attraction. Now, to pretend to tell me that the United States or the Northern States, whichever you please, are going to be frightened from a policy of that kind by our taking upon ourselves great airs, and forming ourselves into a grand Confederation, is to tell me that their people are, like the Chinese, a people to be frightened by loud noises and ugly grimaces. I do not believe they are.

46. THE BRITISH NORTH AMERICA ACT (1867).

Printed in *Federations and Unions within the British Empire*, by H. E. Egerton. Oxford, 1911.

Whereas the Provinces of Canada, Nova Scotia, and New Brunswick have expressed their desire to be federally united into one Dominion under the Crown of the United Kingdom of Great Britain and Ireland, with a Constitution similar in principle to that of the United Kingdom. . . .

3. . . . the Provinces of Canada, Nova Scotia and New

Brunswick shall form and be one Dominion under the name of Canada. . . .

17. There shall be one Parliament for Canada, consisting of the Queen, an Upper House, styled the Senate, and the House of Commons

21. The Senate shall, subject to the provisions of this Act, consist of seventy-two members, who shall be styled Senators.

22. . . . three divisions shall . . . be equally represented in the Senate as follows : Ontario by twenty-four Senators ; Quebec by twenty-four Senators ; and the Maritime Provinces by twenty-four Senators, twelve thereof representing Nova Scotia, and twelve . . . New Brunswick.

24. The Governor-General shall from time to time, in the Queen's name, by Instrument under the Great Seal of Canada, summon qualified persons to the Senate. . . .

29. A Senator shall . . . hold his place in the Senate for life.

37. The House of Commons shall . . . consist of one hundred and eighty-one Members, of whom eighty-two shall be elected for Ontario, sixty-five for Quebec, nineteen for Nova Scotia, and fifteen for New Brunswick.

50. Every House of Commons shall continue for five years from the day of the return of the Writs for choosing the House (subject to be sooner dissolved by the Governor-General) and no longer.

51. On the completion of the census in the year one thousand eight hundred and seventy-one, and of each subsequent decennial census, the representation of the four Provinces shall be readjusted by such authority in such manner, and from such time as the Parliament of Canada from time to time provides, subject and according to the following rules :

1. Quebec shall have the fixed number of sixty-five members.

2. There shall be assigned to each of the other Provinces such a number of Members as will bear the same proportion to the number of its population (ascertained at such census)

as the number sixty-five bears to the number of the population of Quebec (so ascertained) . . .

53. Bills for appropriating any part of the Public Revenue, or for imposing any tax or impost, shall originate in the House of Commons.

54. It shall not be lawful for the House of Commons to adopt or pass any Vote, Resolution, Address, or Bill for the appropriation of any part of the Public Revenue, or of any Tax or Impost, to any purpose, that has not been first recommended to that House by Message of the Governor-General in the Session in which such Vote, Resolution, Address, or Bill is proposed.

58. For each Province there shall be an Officer, styled the Lieutenant-Governor, appointed by the Governor-General in Council by Instrument under the Great Seal of Canada.

60. The salaries of the Lieutenant-Governors shall be fixed and provided by the Parliament of Canada.

91. . . . the exclusive Legislative Authority of the Parliament of Canada extends to all matters coming within the classes of subjects next hereinafter enumerated, that is to say :

(1) The Public Debt and Property ; (2) The regulation of Trade and Commerce ; (3) The raising of money by any mode or system of Taxation ; (4) The borrowing of money on the Public Credit ; (5) Postal Service ; (6) The Census and Statistics ; (7) Militia, Military and Naval Services, and Defence ; (8) The fixing of and providing for the Salaries and Allowances of Civil and other Officers of the Government of Canada ; (9) Beacons, Buoys, Lighthouses, and Sable Island ; (10) Navigation and Shipping ; (11) Quarantine and the establishment and maintenance of Marine Hospitals ; (12) Sea Coast and Inland Fisheries ; (13) Ferries between a Province and any British or Foreign Country, or between two Provinces ; (14) Currency and Coinage ; (15) Banking, Incorporation of Banks, and the issue of Paper Money ; (16) Savings Banks ; (17) Weights and Measures ; (18) Bills of Exchange and Promissory Notes ; (19) Interest ; (20) Legal Tender ; (21) Bankruptcy and Insolvency; (22) Patents of Invention and Discovery ; (23) Copyrights ;

(24) Indians and Lands reserved for the Indians ; (25) Naturalisation and Aliens ; (26) Marriage and Divorce ; (27) The Criminal Law, except the Constitution of the Courts of Criminal Jurisdiction, but including the Procedure in Criminal Matters ; (28) The establishment, maintenance, and management of Penitentiaries ; (29) Such Classes of Subjects as are expressly excepted in the numeration of the Classes of Subjects by this Act assigned exclusively to the Legislatures of the Provinces.

92. In each Province the Legislature may exclusively make laws in relation to matters coming within the classes of subjects next hereinafter enumerated ; that is to say: (1) The amendment . . . of the Constitution of the Province, except as regards the office of Lieutenant-Governor ; (2) Direct taxation within the Province in order to the raising of a revenue for Provincial purposes ; (3) the borrowing of money on the sole credit of the Province ; (4) the establishment and tenure of Provincial offices, and the appointment and payment of Provincial officers ; (5) the management and sale of the Public Lands belonging to the Province, and of the timber and wood thereon ; (6) the establishment, maintenance and management of public and reformatory prisons in and for the Province; (7) the establishment, maintenance and management of Hospitals, Asylums, Charities, and Eleemosynary Institutions in and for the Provinces, other than Marine Hospitals ; (8) Municipal Institutions in the Province ; (9) Shop, Saloon, Tavern, Auctioneer, and other licenses, in order to the raising of a revenue for Provincial, local or municipal purposes ; (10) local works and undertakings [except steamships, railways, canals, telegraphs and other works for the general advantage, or for the advantage of more than one Province] ; (11) the incorporation of Companies with Provincial objects ; (12) the solemnisation of marriage in the Province ; (13) Property and civil rights in the Province ; (14) the administration of justice in the Province [including the maintenance of Provincial courts, civil and criminal, and procedure in civil matters] ; (15) the imposition of punishment by fine, penalty, or imprisonment

[in order to enforce a Provincial law on any of the above matters] ; (16) generally all matters of a merely local or private nature in the Province.

133. Either the English or the French language may be used by any person in the debates of the Houses of the Parliament of Canada and of the Houses of the Legislature of Quebec ; and both those languages shall be used in the respective Records and Journals of those Houses ; and either of those languages may be used by any person or in any pleading or process in or issuing from any Court of Canada established under this Act, and in or from all or any of the Courts of Quebec.

The Acts of the Parliament of Canada and of the Legislature of Quebec shall be printed and published in both those languages.

145. Inasmuch as the Provinces of Canada, Nova Scotia and New Brunswick have joined in a declaration that the construction of the Inter-colonial Railway is essential to the consolidation of the Union of British North America, and to the assent thereto of Nova Scotia and New Brunswick, and have consequently agreed that provision should be made for its immediate construction by the Government of Canada. Therefore, in order to give effect to that agreement, it shall be the duty of the Government and Parliament of Canada to provide for the commencement, within six months after the Union, of a railway connecting the River St. Lawrence with the City of Halifax in Nova Scotia, and for the construction thereof without intermission, and the completion thereof with all practicable speed.

146. It shall be lawful for the Queen, by and with the advice of Her Majesty's Most Honourable Privy Council, on Addresses from the Houses of the Parliament of Canada, and from the Houses of the respective Legislatures of the Colonies or Provinces of Newfoundland, Prince Edward Island, and British Columbia, to admit those Colonies or Provinces, or any of them, into the Union, and on Address from the Houses of the Parliament of Canada to admit Rupert's Land and the

North-Western Territory, or either of them, into the Union, on such terms and conditions in each case as are in the Addresses expressed and as the Queen thinks fit to approve, subject to the provisions of this Act : and the provisions of any Order in Council in that behalf shall have effect as if they had been enacted by the Parliament of the United Kingdom of Great Britain and Ireland.

47. THE WORK OF THE HUDSON BAY COMPANY (to 1869).

Source.—A Paper by Sir Donald Smith (now Lord Strathcona), read to the Royal Colonial Institute in April, 1897. The Company's territories were taken over by the Dominion of Canada in 1869.

The principal business of the Hudson's Bay Company was the purchasing of furs from the Indians, in exchange for arms and ammunition, clothes, and other commodities imported from the United Kingdom. Its prosperity depended upon good relations being maintained with the aborigines. Its officers were able to travel everywhere with freedom and safety, and could rely upon the friendliness of the red men. Advances made to the Indians for their hunting outfits or in times of scarcity were nearly always repaid. On the other hand, the Indians knew that any notes they might receive upon the trading posts, from peripatetic officers a thousand miles away from headquarters, would be honoured on presentation. The foundation of these friendly relations was confidence, and the knowledge the Indians acquired of the white man and his ways during the long administration of the Company made the transfer of the territory to Canada comparatively easy when the time for the surrender arrived. Its policy, which has been followed by successive Governments of Canada, has enabled the country to avoid those Indian wars which were of frequent occurrence in the early days of settlement in the western parts of the United States. Even in the half-breed disturbance in 1869 and 1870 already referred to, and in that of 1885, none of the Indians, with a few exceptions, could be induced to take arms against the forces of law and order. The fur trade over such an immense area was necessarily important; but at the same time, from natural reasons, it was bound to diminish in the more accessible parts where settlement in the future was regarded as possible. There was always a tendency on the part of the Indians to kill as many animals as possible, simply for the skins. They held the belief, some people say, that the more they killed the more rapidly would the animals multiply. Their motives therefore may have been conscientious, but I am afraid they were not altogether unconnected with the prospect of immediate profit. There is not much large game now in the regions traversed by the Canadian Pacific Railway, except perhaps in the more inaccessible districts between the Lakes and Hudson's Bay, and in the territory north and north-west of the river Saskatchewan. The buffalo, which used to furnish the Indian with food, shelter, and raiment, is almost extinct, and it is possible to travel over the prairie for hundreds of miles without seeing any wild animals larger than coyotes and gophers. Deer of various kinds are found occasionally, and bears still less frequently, and it may be said with truth that hunting in Canada, whether for pleasure or for trade, now entails a good deal of hard work. . . .

In former times for trading purposes the unit of value was the beaver skin. The price of everything was calculated at so many skins, and they were the sole medium of exchange. In return for the skins the Indians received pieces of stick prepared in a special manner, each representing a beaver skin, and with these they were able to purchase anything they wanted at the Company's stores. Later on, about 1825, the Company established a paper currency. The highest note was for £1, the next for 5s., and the lowest for 1s. They were known as " Hudson's Bay Blankets," and no fears were ever entertained as to the soundness of the bank. It has been urged against the Hudson's Bay Company that it obstructed the development of the great North-West. On the contrary, it was engaged for two centuries in important pioneer work.

Any corporation of the kind with exclusive privileges and rights was bound to make enemies ; but no single province of Canada could have undertaken the administration or development of the country before confederation, and neither men nor money were available locally to permit of its blossoming out separately as a Colony or as a series of provinces. Whatever may have been the faults of the Company, history will record that its work was for the advantage of the Empire. The Company explored this vast territory, prepared the way for settlement and colonisation, fulfilled an important rôle in the history of Canada, and had not a little to do with the consolidation of the Dominion, and with the development the western country has witnessed in the last thirty years.

48. RED RIVER REBELLION (1870) : ARRIVAL OF THE ENGLISH TROOPS.

Source.—*The Story of a Soldier's Life*, by Field-Marshal Viscount Wolseley. Constable, 1903.

We had looked forward to at least a pretty little field day when our line of skirmishers should enclose Fort Garry and its rebel garrison as in a net. But by early dawn next morning the whole country far and near was a sea of deep and clinging mud. There was then nothing approaching a road in the whole territory, so I had to forgo all pomp and circumstance of war in my final advance and had once more to take to our boats and the dreary oar. We were all wet through, very cold and extremely cross and hungry. A cup of hot tea and a biscuit swallowed quickly for breakfast, and all were again at the oar by 6 a.m., August 24, 1870. The rain poured " in buckets " upon us, and at places the country was under water. . . .

I landed at Point Douglas, only two miles from Fort Garry by road, but six by the river, which there makes a wide bend. A few carts were seized, into which tools and ammunition were transferred, and to two of which the trails of our two small field-pieces were fastened and thus dragged along. The messengers I had sent the previous night into the village round Fort Garry met me here with the assurance that Riel and his gang were still there awaiting anxiously the arrival of Bishop Taché, who was hourly expected. It was confidently asserted that he meant to fight. He had just distributed ammunition—stolen from the Hudson Bay Company's stores —amongst his followers, had had the fort guns loaded, and had closed the gates. I subsequently learned that he and his henchman, a common fellow named Donoghue, had started from Fort Garry during the night to find out where I was and what I was about. But the very heavy rain they encountered was too much for them, and, being afraid of capture by our outposts in the dark, they had gone back to the fort as wise as they had left it.

Our march, though short, was very trying from the heavy rain and the deep mud we had to plough through. But, as all the people we met assured the men we should have a fight, these small and disagreeable drawbacks were ignored.

Fort Garry stands upon the left bank of the Red River, where the Assiniboine falls into it. The fort itself is a high stone-walled square enclosure, with a large circular tower at each of its four corners. The village of Winnipeg—mostly of wooden houses—was nearly half a mile to the north of the fort, and south of it, at about a couple of hundred yards dis- tance, was a boat bridge over the Assiniboine. My object, therefore, was by circling round west of the Fort to obtain possession of that bridge, or at least to command it with my fire. I should then have Riel and company in the right angle inclosed between the two rivers. Our skirmishers in their advance captured a few of Riel's so-called councillors, who were bolting in buggies and other means of conveyance.

As I watched the muzzles of the fort guns, I confess that I hoped each moment to see a flash and to hear a round shot rush by me. I knew they had no shells, and that they did not know how to use them if they had had any. But in the rain, and in the thick atmosphere when the rain ceased for a little, it was difficult to see, even through our glasses, if there were

men at the guns or not. I sent a few officers who had obtained
ponies round the fort to see what was going on in rear of it.
They soon returned with the news that Riel had bolted, and
that the fort gates were open. It was a sad disappointment to
all ranks. . . . But, though we did not catch the fellow, we
had successfully carried out the task that was given us. . . .

We dragged out some of the guns in Fort Garry, upon which
Riel had relied so much, and with them fired a Royal Salute
when the Union Jack was run up the flagstaff. From it had
hung for months before the rebel flag that had been worked
by the nuns of the convent attached to Bishop Taché's
cathedral, and presented by them to Riel.

49. ENTERING THE ROCKIES IN 1872.

Source.—*Ocean to Ocean*, 1873: the diary kept by the Rev. George M.
[1]   Grant, Secretary to the Expedition through Canada of Sandford
Fleming, Engineer-in-Chief of the Canadian Pacific and Inter-
colonial Railways.

September 11th. Away this morning at 6.15 a.m., and
halted at 1 p.m., after crossing the Rivière de Violon or Fiddle
river, when fairly inside the first range. It was a grand morning for mountain scenery. For the first three hours the trail
continued at some distance east from the valley of the Athabasca, among wooded hills, now ascending, now descending,
but on the whole with an upward slope, across creeks where
the ground was invariably boggy, over fallen timber, where
infinite patience was required on the part of horse and man.
Suddenly it opened out on a lakelet, and right in front a semi-
circle of five glorious mountains appeared. . . . For half a
mile down from their summits, no tree, shrub, or plant covered
the nakedness of the three that the old trappers had thought
worthy of names, and a clothing of vegetation would have
marred their massive grandeur. The first three were so near
and towered up so bold that their full forms, even to the long
shadows on them, were reflected clearly in the lakelet, next
to the rushes and spruce of its own shores. . . . The road now

descended rapidly from the summit of the wooded hill that we had so slowly gained, to the valley of the Athabasca. As it wound from point to point among the tall dark green spruces, and over rose bushes and vetches, the soft blue of the mountains gleamed through everywhere; and, when the woods parted, the mighty column of Roche à Perdrix towered above our heads, scuds of clouds kissing its snowy summit. . . . We were entering the magnificent Jasper portals of the Rocky Mountains by a quiet path winding between groves of trees and rich lawns like an English gentleman's park.

. . . Soon the Rivière de Violon was heard brawling round the base of Roche à Perdrix and rushing on like a true mountain torrent to the Athabasca. We stopped to drink to the Queen out of its clear ice-cold waters, and halted for dinner in a grove on the other side of it, thoroughly excited and awed by the grand forms that had begirt our path for the last three hours. We could now sympathise with the daft enthusiast, who returned home after years of absence, and when asked what he had as an equivalent for so much lost time—answered only " I have seen the Rocky Mountains." . . .

There was a delay of three hours at dinner because the horses, as if allured by the genii of the mountains, had wandered more than a mile up the valley, but at four o'clock all was in order again and the march resumed in the same direction. A wooded hill that threw itself out between Roches à Perdrix and à Myette had first to be rounded. This hill narrowed the valley, and forced the trail near the river. When fairly round it, Roche à Myette came full into view, and the trail now led along its base. . . .

As we passed this old warder of the valley, the sun was setting behind Roche Suette. A warm south-west wind as it came in contact with the snowy summit formed heavy clouds, that threw long black shadows, and threatened rain ; but the wind carried them past to empty their buckets on the woods and prairies.

It was time to camp, but where ? The Chief, Beaupré, and Brown rode ahead to see if the river was fordable. The rest followed, going down to the bank and crossing to an island formed by a slew of the river, to avoid a steep rock, the trail along which was fit only for chamois or bighorn. Here we were soon joined by the three who had ridden ahead, and who brought back word that the Athabasca looked ugly, but was still subsiding, and might be fordable in the morning. It was decided to camp on the spot, and send the horses back a mile for feed. The resources of the island would not admit of our light cotton sheet being stretched as an overhead shelter, so we selected the lee side of a dwarf aspen thicket, and spread our blankets on the gravel, a good fire being made in front to cook our supper and keep our feet warm through the night. Some of us sat up late, watching the play of the moonlight on the black clouds that drifted about her troubled face, as she hung over Roche Jacques ; and then we stretched ourselves out to sleep on our rough but truly enviable couch, rejoicing in the open sky for a canopy and in the circle of great mountains that formed the walls of our indescribably magnificent bed chamber. It had been a day long to be remembered.

50. THE DESTINY OF CANADA (1873).

Source.—*Ocean to Ocean.* (Cf. 49.)

From the sea-pastures and coal-fields of Nova Scotia and the forests of New Brunswick, almost from historic Louisbourg up the St. Lawrence to historic Quebec; through the great province of Ontario, and on lakes that are really seas; by copper and silver mines so rich as to recall stories of the Arabian Nights, though only the rim of the land has been explored; on the chain of lakes, where the Ojibbeway is at home in his canoe, to the great plains, where the Cree is equally at home on his horse; through the prairie Province of Manitoba, and rolling meadows and park-like country, equally fertile, out of which a dozen Manitobas shall be carved in the next quarter of a century; along the banks of

> A full-fed river winding slow
> By herds upon an endless plain,

full-fed from the exhaustless glaciers of the Rocky Mountains, and watering " the great lone land "; over illimitable coal measures and deep woods ; on to the mountains, which open their gates, more widely than to our wealthier neighbours, to lead us to the Pacific ; down deep gorges filled with mighty timber, and rivers whose ancient deposits are gold beds, sands like those of Pactolus and channels choked with fish ; on to the many harbours of mainland and island, that look right across to the old Eastern Thule " with its rosy pearls and golden-roofed palaces," and open their arms to welcome the swarming millions of Cathay ; over all this we had travelled, and it was all our own.

> Where's the coward that would not dare
> To fight for such a land ?

Thank God, we have a country. It is not our poverty of land or sea, of wood or mine, that shall ever urge us to be traitors. But the destiny of a country depends not on its material resources. It depends on the character of its people. Here, too, is full ground for confidence. We in everything " are sprung of earth's first blood, have titles manifold." We come of a race that never counted the number of its foes, nor the number of its friends, when freedom, loyalty or God was concerned.

Two courses are possible, though it is almost an insult to say there are two, for the one requires us to be false to our traditions and history, to our future and to ourselves. A third course has been hinted at ; but only dreamers or emasculated intellects would seriously propose " Independence " to four millions of people, face to face with thirty-eight millions. Some one may have even a fourth to propose. The Abbé Sieyès had a cabinet filled with pigeon-holes, in each of which was a cut-and-dried Constitution for France. *Doctrinaires* fancy that at any time they can say " Go to, let us make a Constitution," and that they can fit it on a nation as readily as new coats on their backs. There never was a profounder mistake. A nation grows, and its Constitution must grow

with it. The nation cannot be pulled up by the roots, cannot
be dissociated from its past, without danger to its highest
interests. Loyalty is essential to the fulfilment of a distinc-
tive mission—essential to its true glory. Only one course,
therefore, is possible for us, consistent with the self-respect
that alone gains the respect of others ; to seek, in the consolidation of the Empire, a common Imperial citizenship, with
common responsibilities and a common inheritance.

51. TARIFF REFORM IN CANADA IN 1876.

Source.—A Speech by Sir John A. Macdonald, quoted in the *Life*, by
G. R. Parkin, in "The Makers of Canada" series.

We are in favour of a tariff that will incidentally give protection to our manufacturers ; that will develop our manufacturing industries. We believe that that can be done, and, if
done, it will give a home market to our farmers. The farmers
will be satisfied when they know that large bodies of operatives are working in the mills and manufactories in every village
and town in the country. They know that every man of them
is a consumer, and that he must have pork and flour, beef and
all that the farmers raise, and they know that, instead of being
obliged to send their grain to a foreign and uncertain market,
they will have a market at their own door. And the careful
housewife, every farmer's wife, will know that everything that
is produced under her care—the poultry, the eggs, the butter
and the garden stuff—will find a ready and profitable market
in the neighbouring town and village.

No country is great with only one industry. Agriculture is
our most important, but it cannot be our only staple. All men
are not fit to be farmers ; there are men with mechanical and
manufacturing genius who desire to become operatives or
manufacturers of some kind, and we must have means to
employ them ; and when there is a large body of successful
and prosperous manufacturers, the farmer will have a home
market for his produce, and the manufacturer a home market

for his goods, and we shall have nothing to fear. And therefore I have been urging upon my friends that we must lay aside all old party quarrels about old party doings. Those old matters are matters before the flood, which have gone by and are settled for ever, many of them settled by governments of which I was a member. Why should parties divide on these old quarrels ? Let us divide on questions affecting the present and future interests of the country.

The question of the day is that of the protection of our farmers from the unfair competition of foreign produce, and the protection of our manufacturers. I am in favour of reciprocal free trade if it can be obtained ; but, so long as the policy of the United States closes the markets to our products, we should have a policy of our own as well, and consult only our own interests. That subject wisely and vigorously dealt with, you will see confidence restored, the present depression dispelled, and the country prosperous and contented.

52. PRAIRIE GREYHOUNDS.

POEM BY E. PAULINE JOHNSON.

The Canadian Pacific Railway was completed in November, 1885.

(1) *C.P.R. Westbound.*

I swing to the sunset land,
The world of prairie, the world of plain,
The world of promise and hope and gain,
The world of gold and the world of grain,
And the world of the willing hand.

I carry the brave and bold,
The one who works for the nation's bread,
The one whose past is a thing that's dead,
The one who battles and beats ahead,
And the one who goes for gold.

I swing to the land to be :
I am the power that laid its floors,
I am the guide to its western stores,
I am the key to its golden doors,
That open alone to me.

(2) *C.P.R. Eastbound.*

I swing to the land of morn,
The grey old east with its grey old seas,
The land of leisure, the land of ease,
The land of flowers and fruits and trees,
And the place where we were born.

Freighted with wealth I come,—
Food and fortune ; and fellow that went
Far out west on adventure bent,
With well-worn pick and a folded tent,
Is bringing his bullion home.

I never will be renowned
As my twin that swings to the western marts,
For I am she of the humbler parts ;
But I am the joy of the waiting hearts,
For I am the homeward-bound !

53. LAURIER'S TRIBUTE TO MACDONALD (1891).

Source.—Sir Wilfred Laurier's Speech in the Canadian House of Commons on the death of Sir John Macdonald : Canadian Hansard, 8th June, 1891, quoted in part in J. S. Willison's *Sir Wilfred Laurier and the Liberal Party* ; and in part also in G. R. Parkin's *Sir John A. Macdonald.*

The place of Sir John Macdonald in this country was so large and so absorbing that it is almost impossible to conceive that the political life of this country, the fate of this country, can continue without him. . . . I think it can be asserted that, for the supreme art of governing men, Sir John Macdonald was gifted as few men in any land or in any age were gifted—gifted with the highest of all qualities, qualities which would have made him famous wherever exercised, and which would have shone all the more conspicuously the larger the theatre. The fact that he could congregate together elements the most heterogeneous and blend them into one compact party, and to the end of his life keep them steadily under his hand, is perhaps altogether unprecedented. The fact that during all those years he retained unimpaired not only the confidence, but the devotion—the ardent devotion—and affection of his party, is evidence that, besides those higher qualities of statesmanship to which we were daily witnesses, he was also endowed with those inner, subtle, undefinable graces of soul which win and keep the hearts of men. . . .

He was fond of power and he never made any secret of it. Many times we have heard him avow it on the floor of this Parliament, and his ambition in this respect was gratified as perhaps no other man's ambition ever was. In my judgment even the career of William Pitt can hardly compare with that of Sir John Macdonald in this respect ; for although William Pitt, moving in a higher sphere, had to deal with problems greater than our problems, yet I doubt if in the intricate management of a party William Pitt had to contend with difficulties equal to those that Sir John Macdonald had to contend with.

As to his statesmanship, it is written in the history of Canada. It may be said without any exaggeration whatever, that the life of Sir John Macdonald, from the date he entered Parliament, is the history of Canada: for he was connected and associated with all the events, all the facts which brought Canada from the position it then occupied—the position of two small provinces, having nothing in common but their common allegiance, united by a bond of paper, and united by nothing else—to the present state of development which Canada has reached. Although my political views compel me to say that, in my judgment, his actions were not always the best that could have been taken in the interest of Canada, although my conscience compels me to say that of late he has imputed to his opponents motives which I must say in my heart he has misconceived, yet I am only too glad here to sink these differences, and to remember only the great services he has performed for our country—to remember that his actions always displayed great originality of view, unbounded fertility of resource, a high level of intellectual conception, and, above all, a far-reaching vision beyond the event of the day, and still higher, permeating the whole, a broad patriotism—a devotion to Canada's welfare, Canada's advancement, and Canada's glory.

54. THE CANADIAN TROOPS IN THE BOER WAR (1900).

Source.—Speech by Sir Wilfred Laurier in the Canadian House of Commons, 13th March, 1900 ; quoted in J. S. Willison's *Sir Wilfred Laurier and the Liberal Party.*

We were not forced by England, we were not forced by Mr. Chamberlain or by Downing Street, to do what we did, and I cannot conceive what my honourable friend meant when he said that the future of this country was not to be pledged by this Government.   When and where did we pledge the future of this country ?   We acted in the full independence of our sovereign power.   What we did we did of our own free will, but I am not to answer for the consequences or for what will take place in the future.   My honourable friend says that the consequence is that we will be called on to take part in other wars.   I have only this to answer to my honourable friend, that, if it should be the will of the people of Canada at any future stage to take part in any war of England, the people of Canada will have to have their way.   Let me say to my honourable friend further, the maxim which he has advocated this afternoon, and which he took from the despatch of Lord Grey to Lord Elgin, " It must be remembered that the government of the British Colonies in North America cannot be carried on in opposition to the will of the people," was the language in 1847, it holds good in 1900, and will be the language used so long as we have free parliamentary institutions in Canada. But I have no hesitation in saying to my honourable friend that if, as a consequence of our action to-day, the doctrine were to be admitted that Canada should take part in all the wars of Great Britain and contribute to the military expenditure of the Empire, I will agree with him that we should revise the conditions of things existing between us and Great Britain. If we were to be compelled to take part in all the wars of Britain, I have no hesitation in saying that I agree with my honourable friend that, sharing the burden, we should also share the responsibility. Under that condition of things, which does not exist, we should have the right to say to Great Britain " If you want us to help you, you must call us to your councils ; if you want us to take part in wars, let us share not only the burdens, but the responsibilities as well." But there is no occasion to say that to-day. . . .

. . . We were not compelled to do what we did, but if we chose to be generous, to do a little more than we were bound to do, where is a man living who would find fault with us for that action ? He dreads the consequences of this action in sending out a military contingent to South Africa. Let me tell him from the bottom of my heart that my heart is full of the hopes I entertain of the beneficial results which will accrue from that action. . . . When the telegraph brought us the news that such was the good impression made by our volunteers that the Commander-in-Chief had placed them in the post of honour, in the first rank, to share the danger with that famous corps, the Gordon Highlanders ; when we heard that they had justified fully the confidence placed in them, that they had charged like veterans, that their conduct was heroic and had won for them the encomiums of the Commander-in-Chief and the unstinted admiration of their comrades, who had faced death upon a hundred battlefields in all parts of the world, is there a man whose bosom did not swell with pride, that noblest of all pride, that pride of pure patriotism, the pride of the consciousness of our rising strength, the pride of the consciousness that on that day it had been revealed to the world that a new power had arisen in the West?

Nor is that all. The work of union and harmony between the chief races of this country is not yet complete. We know by the unfortunate occurrences that took place only last week that there is much to do in that way. But there is no bond of union so strong as the bond created by common dangers faced in common. To-day there are men in South Africa representing the two branches of the Canadian family fighting side by side for the honour of Canada. Already some of them have fallen, giving to the country the last full measure of devotion. Their remains have been laid in the same grave, there to remain to the end of time in that last fraternal embrace. Can we not hope, I ask my honourable friend himself, that in that grave shall be buried the last vestiges of our former antagonism? If such shall be the result, if we can indulge that hope, if we can believe that in that grave shall be buried contentions, the sending of the contingents would be the greatest service ever rendered Canada since Confederation.

55. PIONEERS OF THE RAILWAY (1910).

Source.—*The Making of a Great Canadian Railway*, by Frederick A. Talbot. London, 1912. (The story of the Grand Trunk Pacific Railway.)

The swamp occasioned many anxious nights, and much burning of midnight oil. At places it appeared to be bottomless. The ballast locomotive would haul train after trainload of spoil excavated from the ballast-pit, and push it cautiously along to the end of the dump, where the trucks would be discharged. The rubble would rush down the declivity, and as it came into contact with the surface of the morass there would be a wicked squelch. Then the bog would open, and slowly, but surely and silently, the discharged mass would disappear into the viscous mass until the last vestige had slipped from sight, and the slime had rolled over the spot, concealing all evidences of the few hundred tons of material emptied on to the spot but a few minutes before. The engineer would sound the bog anxiously for signs of the bottom. Yes, he could feel it all right—10, 15, perhaps 20 feet below the surface. The trains would continue to rattle up and down with heavily laden trucks, and send the contents crashing pell-mell into the swamp below. Ten train-loads of gravel, rock, and what not would disappear from sight, and the engineer would probe the treacherous sponge once more. But the soundings did not vary a foot. Where had the dump gone ? The ballast had sunk simply to the bottom of the bog, and had spread itself out on all sides, finding its own level like water. The bed of the morass was as broken as the hill-side near by, and was intersected in all directions by ruts and gullies. Until these holes were filled, there could be no possible hope of the embankment appearing above the surface of the bog. . . .

While the upper stretches of New Ontario and Quebec were occasioning the engineers many anxious moments, owing to the eccentricities of the muskeg and swamp, the graders advancing eastwards from Winnipeg were in close grips with rock, which offered a most stubborn resistance. . . .

For hour after hour, day after day, month after month, nothing was heard but the chink-chink of drills and the devastating roar of explosive with its splitting and disintegrating work. Advance was exceedingly slow, some of the blasts requiring as much as six weeks or more to prepare, and then only breaking up sufficient of the granite mass to permit of an advance of about 200 feet. . . .

It was on work of this nature where the greatest number of accidents occurred, the majority of which might have been avoided had the men engaged in the operations displayed but ordinary care. . . . Dynamite was responsible for more deaths on this undertaking than any other accident—the collapse of the Quebec Bridge notwithstanding—and sickness combined. . . .

The slush on the lakes was one of the greatest obstacles which those in the field were doomed to face. From the bank it looks safe enough, but to venture upon its surface is to court certain death. Why? It is very simple to explain. The lakes freeze up under the advance of winter, but before the encrustation has assumed a sufficient thickness there is a heavy fall of snow. Under the weight of the white, fleecy mantle the ice slowly and steadily sinks below the level of the water, which, pouring over the mirror-like armour, saturates the snow. Under successive falls of snow the ice sinks lower and lower, and the slush assumes a greater and greater thickness, until at last it measures from 4 or 6 to 10 feet in depth. What is more, it persistently refuses to freeze. The appearance of its smooth surface tempts the daring to advance. It withstands his weight until he has ventured a fair distance from the shore; then, without the slightest warning, suddenly it opens up, drawing the unwary into its icy depths, where he is soon suffocated. One cannot escape from its embrace, no matter how great the struggle, and, when the end is reached, the slush gathers over one, giving no inkling of the ghastly secret beneath. . . .

The greatest summer peril was from bush fires, which rage with terrific fury and are of frequent occurrence throughout New Ontario, the spruce, jack-pine and other indigenous resinous trees providing excellent fuel for the flames. The danger from this terror of the forest was not so much in regard to human life, as to the destruction of precious provisions hauled in and cached for the succeeding winter, the loss of which might have jeopardised the welfare of a whole survey party. Once this devastating fiend secures a firm grip it roars viciously. The forest through which it sweeps with incredible speed becomes a fiendish furnace, which either has to burn itself out, or to suffer extinction by a tropical downpour of rain.

56. CANADIAN NAVAL POLICY (1912).

Source.—*The Times* Special Supplement, 31st December, 1912—
a Review of the Year 1912.

Mr. Borden's main proposal was that a sum of £7,000,000 should be voted at once for the construction of three armoured ships of the latest and strongest type. These ships were to be built in England and placed at the disposal of the Admiralty, subject to recall at a later period should the permanent naval policy of the Dominion require it. To show their origin they were to bear Canadian names, and they were to be additional to the programme of construction already laid down for next year's Navy Estimates by the First Lord of the Admiralty. In order, meanwhile, that naval shipbuilding should make a start in Canada, yards were to be established for the construction of certain cruisers and auxiliary craft which the Admiralty engaged to order from the Dominion. A very important step towards closer consultation in matters of policy was, moreover, announced in the appointment of a Canadian Minister to the Committee of Defence. This Minister was to have the right of being present at all meetings of the Committee, which would thus be brought much more closely in touch with the Dominion Cabinet. In the course of his speech, Mr. Borden also read out an extremely lucid and well-worded Memorandum on the growth of foreign navies, with which he had been supplied at his own especial request by the Admiralty.

The main effect of the Memorandum was to show the increasing concentration in home waters demanded of the British Navy by the swift expansion of the German Fleet and the consequent reduction of Imperial naval strength in all outlying seas. The statement was an eloquent corollary to a suggestion thrown out by Mr. Churchill on May 16 at a banquet of the Shipwrights' Company. The First Lord then urged that, while Great Britain made herself responsible for the security of the Empire in the central European theatre, the Dominions might combine to patrol the outer seas. This argument was strongly developed by Mr. Borden in the course of his speech ; and, though it has not been repeated by Mr. Churchill, it is likely to exercise a very important influence on the development of opinion on the naval question in the Dominions. Mr. Borden's proposals were received with enthusiasm in this country ; but Liberal critics showed a tendency to question the constitutional propriety of the addition to the Committee

C. H

of Defence, and to complain of the cost of manning and maintaining ships which were to be strictly additional to those already demanded by the Admiralty. The latter line of complaint, though never at all widely urged, received some reinforcement from Sir Wilfred Laurier's speech a week later. The Leader of the Opposition supported, as we have already said, the vote of £7,000,000 ; but he moved an amendment to the Bill proposing that this sum should be devoted to the construction of a Canadian Navy, to be manned and maintained entirely by the Dominion. It was added that the ships proposed should be built in the Dominion and should form two separate fleet-units, one on the Atlantic and one on the Pacific Coast. Sir Wilfred Laurier also took occasion to reiterate a view formerly expressed that Dominion ships should not take part in any Imperial war except upon a vote of the Canadian Parliament. . . .

It would, however, be leaving the most significant part of the event untold not to record the profound impression which it has created throughout the Empire. The gift of the Malay States had already roused a strong wave of Imperial sentiment when Mr. Borden delivered his speech. It is no exaggeration to say that the Canadian initiative was hailed with fervid enthusiasm everywhere. Opinions differed in regard to the details of control, but there was only one voice regarding the main proposal of three first-class ships. Great attention was, moreover, given to the announcement that a Canadian Minister should in future be regularly summoned to the Committee of Defence, and the opinion was freely expressed that in the proposal lay the germ of a much closer future union in foreign policy and defence.

57. CANADIAN STREAMS.

By CHARLES G. D. ROBERTS.

O rivers rolling to the sea
From lands that bear the maple tree,
How swell your voices with the strain
Of loyalty and liberty !

A holy music heard in vain
By coward heart and sordid brain,
To whom this strenuous being seems
Naught but a greedy race for gain.

O unsung streams—not splendid themes
You lack to fire your patriot dreams !
Annals of glory gild your waves,
Hope freights your tides, Canadian streams !

St. Lawrence, whose wide water laves
The shores that ne'er have nourished slaves !
Swift Richelieu of lilied fame !
Niagara of glorious graves !

Thy rapids, Ottawa, proclaim
Where Daulac and his heroes came !
Thy tides, St. John, declare La Tour,
And, later, many a loyal name !

Thou inland stream, whose vales, secure
From storm, Tecumseh's death made poor !
And thou, small water, red with war,
'Twixt Beaubassin and Beauséjour !

Dread Saguenay, where eagles soar,
What voice shall from the bastioned shore
The tale of Roberval reveal
Or his mysterious fate deplore ?

Annapolis, do thy floods yet feel
Faint memories of Champlain's keel,
Thy pulses yet the deed repeat
Of Poutrincourt and D'Iberville.

And thou far tide, whose plains now beat
With march of myriad westering feet,
Saskatchewan, whose virgin sod
So late Canadian blood made sweet ?

Your bulwark hills, your valleys broad,
Streams where De Salaberry trod,
Where Wolfe achieved, where Brock was slain,
Their voices are the voice of God !

O sacred waters ! not in vain,
Across Canadian height and plain,
Ye sound us in triumphant tone
The summons of your high refrain.

NOTES

LORD DUFFERIN (Frederick Blackwood), 1826-92 : Governor-General of Canada, 1872-8.

JACQUES CARTIER, 1491-1557 : explored the St. Lawrence, 1535-42.

COUNT DE MONTS, 1560-1611 : a Huguenot gentleman of the French Court, had a patent for the colonisation of Acadia (Nova Scotia) from 1603 to 1607.

SAMUEL CHAMPLAIN, 1567-1635 : interested in Canada, 1603-35 : founded Quebec, 1608.

THOMAS JAMES, 1593-1635 : a Bristol man.

LUKE FOX, 1586-1635 : sailed from London.

SIEUR DE MAISONNEUVE : founder of Montreal and Governor there for 22 years : died in 1676.

CHARLES DE MONTMAGNY : Governor of Canada, 1636-48, was opposed to the settlement of Montreal.

COUNT DE FRONTENAC, 1620-98 : Governor of Canada, 1672-82 and 1689-98. The strongest Governor during the French period.

FRANCIS PARKMAN, 1823-93 : the most picturesque of American historians : accurate as well as graphic.

MADELAINE VERCHÈRES : born 1678, married a second time in 1722, date of death unknown.

LOUIS-HECTOR DE CALLIÈRES, 1646-1703 : came to Canada as Governor of Montreal in 1684 : Governor-General at Quebec, 1699.

GILLES HOCQUART : Intendant of New France, 1731-48 : an energetic and able official.

SIEUR DE LA VÉRENDRYE, 1685-1749 : explored to the west of Canada, 1731-8. His sons are said to have sighted the Rockies in 1742.

MAJOR CHARLES LAWRENCE administered the government of Nova Scotia from 1753, became officially Governor in 1756 : died in 1760.

HORACE WALPOLE, 1717-97 : son of Sir Robert Walpole : wrote several books, but is most famous for his letters. Most of the letters here quoted were written to Sir Horace Mann, the British envoy at Florence.

HENRY SEYMOUR CONWAY, 1721-95 : was a soldier and statesman, who had been much criticised for his failure in an expedition to Rochfort in 1757.

LORD HOLDERNESS (Robert D'Arcy), 1718-78 : Secretary of State, 1751-61.

JAMES WOLFE, 1727-59 : military commander of the Quebec expedition of 1759. On his death, George Townshend, 1724-1807, succeeded to the command at Quebec. He returned to England and left the defence to James Murray, 1719-94. The commander-in-chief in N. America was Jeffrey Amherst, 1717-97. The Admiral at Quebec was Sir Charles Saunders, 1713-75.

MARQUIS DE MONTCALM, 1712-59 : French General in North America, 1756-9.

SAMUEL HEARNE, 1745-92 : made the first inland explorations undertaken by the Hudson Bay Company, 1770-5.

SIR ALEXANDER MACKENZIE, 1755-1820 : explored the Mackenzie river, 1789, and crossed the Rockies to the Pacific in 1793. Captain George Vancouver, R.N., 1758-98, was exploring the coast at the same time.

LOUIS RODRIGUE MASSON, 1833-1903 : a member of the Canadian Senate and Lieut.-Governor of Quebec, collected and published narratives by a number of traders in the service of the North-West Company.

GEORGE HERIOT, 1766-1844 : born in Jersey, became Postmaster-General of Canada : was second in command at the battle of Chateauguay in the War of 1812.

SIMON FRASER, 1776-1862 : explored the Fraser river in 1808 : declined knighthood in 1811 : died poor near Montreal.

JAMES FITZGIBBON, 1780-1863 : born in Ireland : won the battle of Beaver Dam, 1813 : helped to put down the rebellion in Upper Canada, 1837 : returned to England later.

SIR PHINEAS RIALL, 1775-1850 : commanded at the battle of Chippawa : Governor of Grenada, 1816 : knighted, 1833.

SIR GORDON DRUMMOND, 1771-1854 : born at Quebec : fought as colonel against the French in Egypt, 1801 : won the battle of Lundy's Lane, 1814 : administrator of Lower Canada, 1815-6.

LORD SELKIRK (Thomas Douglas), 1771-1820 : planted a colony in Prince Edward Island in 1803 : his colonists on the Red River, 1815-6, twice driven out by the North-West Company, but restored in 1817.

ROBERT SEMPLE, 1766-1816 : born at Boston : travelled widely : became Governor of the Hudson Bay Company's territories in 1815.

CUTHBERT GRANT, the leader of the attacking party, was a Scottish half-breed.

JOHN GALT, 1779-1839 : best known as a Scots novelist : visited Canada in the interests of the Canada Company in 1824 and 1826-9.

THOMAS CHANDLER HALIBURTON, 1796-1865 : a Nova Scotian : Judge of
the Supreme Court there : in *Sam Slick* posed as a Connecticut
clockmaker pointing out the foibles and want of initiative of the
Nova Scotians : founded the American school of humour : later
came to England, and was a Member of Parliament, 1859-65.

LORD DURHAM (John George Lambton), 1792-1840 : radical member
of Parliament : helped to prepare the Reform Bill : son-in-law of
Earl Grey, who carried the Bill : ambassador to Russia, Prussia,
and Austria : sent as Special Commissioner to Canada after the
rebellion of 1837 : his Report is a " State paper on colonial affairs
which will live to all time " (Sir Charles Lucas).

JOSEPH HOWE, 1804-73 : a distinguished Nova Scotian statesman, who
led the movement for responsible government in his native province :
became Lieut.-Governor of N.S., 1873.

LORD JOHN RUSSELL, 1792-1878 : son of the sixth Duke of Bedford :
whig statesman : Home Secretary, 1835 : Colonial Secretary, 1839 :
Prime Minister, 1846 : Foreign Secretary, 1852 : Lord President of
the Council, 1854 : Colonial Secretary, 1855 : Foreign Secretary,
1859 : Prime Minister, 1865. The most important period in his
career is probably that of his ministry from 1846 to 1852.

SIR GEORGE SIMPSON, 1792-1860 : Governor of the Hudson Bay Company's territories, 1821-60 : crossed North America, 1828 : made
" overland " journey round the world, 1841-2.

JOHN ROBERT GODLEY, 1814-61 : much interested in colonisation :
helped to found the Church of England Colony of Canterbury in
New Zealand, 1850 : later became Under Secretary at War.

LORD ELGIN (James Bruce), 1811-63 : Governor of Jamaica, 1842 :
Governor-General of Canada, 1847-54 : carried out Lord Durham's
plan of responsible government—he was Durham's son-in-law :
envoy to China, 1857-8 and 1860-1 : Viceroy of India, 1862-3.

SIR GEORGE GREY (1799-1882), who was Colonial Secretary, 1854-5,
and several times Home Secretary, was a nephew of the Earl Grey
who carried the Reform Act. He must not be confused with the
more famous Sir George Grey (1812-98), who was Governor of South
Australia, of New Zealand, and of Cape Colony.

SIR JOHN A. MACDONALD, 1815-91 : born at Kingston, Ontario :
leader of his (Conservative) party, 1856-91 : led the federation
movement, and became the first Prime Minister of the Dominion :
politically responsible for the construction of the Canadian Pacific
Railway : Prime Minister, 1878-91.

GEORGE BROWN, 1818-80 : founder and editor of the Toronto *Globe* :
leader of the radical party, but formed a coalition with Macdonald
in order to carry Confederation, resigning as soon as success was
assured.

CHRISTOPHER DUNKIN, 1811-81 : born in London, England : went to Canada, 1836 : he was at first an opponent, but later a strong supporter, of Confederation : passed the Canada Temperance Act : became a Judge of the Supreme Court of Quebec.

LORD STRATHCONA (Donald Smith), born in 1820 in Elginshire : entered the service of the Hudson Bay Co. in 1838 : Governor of its territories, 1868 : on the rebellion at the Red River in 1870, he succeeded in maintaining peace until the arrival of troops under Lord Wolseley : financially responsible for the making of the
✓ Canadian Pacific Railway : Governor of the Hudson Bay Co. in London, 1889 : raised to the peerage, 1897.

GARNET, LORD WOLSELEY, 1833-1913 : Commander-in-Chief of the British Army, 1895-1900 : served in the Crimea and in India and China : commanded in Ashanti and Egypt as well as in the Red River expedition.

GEORGE MONRO GRANT, 1835-1902 : Principal of Queen's University, Kingston, 1877 : President of the Imperial Federation League, Ontario, 1889.

MISS E. PAULINE JOHNSON, " Tekahionwake," the descendant of Indian chiefs, who were the loyal allies of the British, has published several volumes of Canadian poetry.

SIR WILFRED LAURIER, born 1841, in Quebec : leader of the Liberal party, 1887 : Prime Minister, 1896-1911.

ROBERT LAIRD BORDEN, born 1854, in Nova Scotia : leader of the Conservative party, 1901 : Prime Minister, 1911.

CHARLES G. D. ROBERTS, Canadian poet, historian and novelist, born in New Brunswick, 1860 : has been a Professor in Nova Scotia and an editor in New York.

GLASGOW : PRINTED AT THE UNIVERSITY PRESS BY ROBERT MACLEHOSE AND CO. LTD.

Bell's English History Source-Books

JOINT EDITORS

S. E. WINBOLT, M.A., Christ's Hospital, Horsham

KENNETH BELL, M.A., Fellow of All Souls College, Oxford

THE FOLLOWING VOLUMES ARE READY

1154-1216. The Angevins and the Charter. Edited by S. M. TOYNE, M.A.

1307-1399. War and Misrule. Edited by A. LOCKE.

1485-1547. The Reformation and the Renaissance. Edited by FRED W. BEWSHER, B.A.

1547-1603. The Age of Elizabeth. Edited by ARUNDELL ESDAILE, M.A.

1603-1660. Puritanism and Liberty. Edited by KENNETH BELL, M.A.

1660-1714. A Constitution in Making. Edited by G. B. PERRETT, M.A.

1714-1760. Walpole and Chatham. Edited by K. A. ESDAILE.

1760-1801. American Independence and the French Revolution. Edited by S. E. WINBOLT, M.A.

1801-1815. England and Napoleon. Edited by S. E. WINBOLT, M.A.

1815-1837. Peace and Reform. Edited by A. C. EDWARDS.

1876-1887. Imperialism and Mr. Gladstone. Edited by R. H. GRETTON.

Other Volumes in Preparation

THE method adopted in this series is now recognized by the most progressive teachers as an invaluable aid to the rational study of history.

Up till now no material for teaching on these lines has been available in a sufficiently cheap and handy form. It is hoped that the issue of the volumes at 1s. net will put them within the reach of every type of school.

LONDON: G. BELL AND SONS, LTD.

Crown 8vo. With Maps and Plans. Second Edition. 2s.

An Introduction to English Industrial History

By HENRY ALLSOPP, B.A., Late Vice-Principal of Ruskin College, Oxford

THIS book attempts to make a really interesting, simple and suggestive introduction to industrial and economic history. It is intended to induce our young men and women of all classes to study earnestly this important subject, which has, up to the present, been impossible, because the text-books are too expensive or else too learned and academic.

Contents: Part I. THE MANORIAL SYSTEM. Part II. TOWNS AND GUILDS. Part III. STATE REGULATION AND THE MERCANTILE SYSTEM. Part IV. THE INDUSTRIAL REVOLUTION.

Mediaeval England
A FRAMEWORK OF ENGLISH HISTORY
1066-1485

By S. M. TOYNE, M.A., Late Senior History Master at Haileybury College. 1s.

IT is suggested that this volume may be of considerable assistance not only to students using the ordinary text-books, but also to those whose work is based on some such series as Messrs. Bell's English History Source Books. The author's object has been to produce a volume that will be an aid to, and not a substitute for, reading, and it is hoped that it may be of value as giving a summary of important events and a review of national development.

Crown 8vo. 1s.

Civil Service History Questions

Edited by A. PERCIVAL NEWTON, M.A.
Assistant Master at the Strand School

THE questions contained in this volume have been selected from History Papers set to candidates for positions in the middle grades of the Civil Service and in the Army, Navy, and Indian Police. It has been designed in such a way as to provide types of almost every question set. A selection of questions on General European History has been given at the end of the book.

LONDON: G. BELL AND SONS, LTD.

EUROPE SINCE 1815. By CHARLES D.

HAZEN, Professor in Smith College. New and cheaper
edition. 10s. 6d. net.

". . . Professor Hazen's book is a veritable store of sound political wisdom for
the student of history, and at the same time is written in a lively style, full of the
actual thoughts and words of great historical personages."—*Journal of Education.*

ATLAS OF EUROPEAN HISTORY. By

EARLE W. Dow, Professor in the University of Michigan.
8vo. 6s. net.

This work contains thirty-two double-page coloured maps and
eighteen smaller maps, plans, etc., in black and white. The maps
cover the field of European History from the Ancient Eastern Empires
to the Decline of Europe in the Americas and Contemporary Europe.
It meets the need of a handy historical atlas in the English language
suitable for use in schools and colleges. The full index adds to its
value.

MEDIÆVAL EUROPE, 395-1270. By

CHARLES BÉMONT and G. MONOD. Translated under the
Editorship of GEORGE BURTON ADAMS, Professor in Yale
University. Crown 8vo. 6s. 6d. net.

THE HISTORY OF THE MIDDLE

AGES. By VICTOR DURUY, of the French Academy.
Translated from the Twelfth Edition by E. H. and M. D.
WHITNEY. With Notes and Revisions by GEORGE BURTON
ADAMS, Professor of History at Yale University. Crown 8vo.
6s. 6d. net.

A HISTORY OF MODERN EUROPE.

From the Fall of Constantinople. By THOMAS HENRY
DYER, LL.D. Third Edition, revised and continued to
the end of the Nineteenth Century, by ARTHUR HASSALL,
M.A., Student of Christ Church, Oxford. In Six Volumes.
Crown 8vo. With Maps. 3s. 6d. each.

" For the general reader, and even for the historical student who is content with
anything short of original research, Dyer's book is indispensable, at any rate for
the first three centuries after the fall of Constantinople. But if it was to keep its
place as a text-book, it was unavoidable that it should be submitted to a somewhat
drastic revision in the light of additions made to our knowledge since it first
appeared. This work could not have been committed to more competent hands
than Mr. Arthur Hassall."—*St. James's Gazette.*

LONDON: G. BELL AND SONS, LTD.

Bell's History Course

IN THREE VOLUMES

BOOK I.—FOR JUNIOR CLASSES

First Lessons in English History. Crown 8vo. 102 pages. With numerous Illustrations. 10*d*.

BOOK II.—FOR MIDDLE CLASSES

A Junior History of England. By E. NIXON, late Head Mistress of Junior School, Specialist in History, Ladies' College, Cheltenham. Third Edition. Crown 8vo. 254 pages. With 66 Illustrations. 1*s*. 6*d*.

"This Junior History of England is written in simple and telling language, and gives an admirable outline of the development and growth of England. Illustrations, chiefly portraits, are from contemporary sources, and therefore specially interesting."—*Educational News.*

BOOK III.—FOR SENIOR CLASSES

A Senior History of England. By A. E. McKILLIAM, M.A., University of St. Andrews. Crown 8vo. With numerous Illustrations. 2*s*.

Landmarks in the History of Europe. By E. M. RICHARDSON, B.A., Assistant Mistress of St. Saviour's and St. Olave's Grammar School for Girls, S. E. Crown 8vo. Third Edition. With many Illustrations and Maps. 2*s*.

History of England. By JOHN LINGARD, D.D. New and cheaper revised edition brought down to the Reign of King George V, by DOM HENRY NORBERT BIRT, O.S.B. With a Preface by ABBOT GASQUET, D.D. With Maps. Third Edition. Large crown 8vo. 640 pages. 3*s*. 6*d*. Or in 2 vols.: Vol. I (to 1485), 2*s*.; Vol. II (1485-1913), 2*s*.

"That Dom Norbert Birt's volume has really given us what was needed we have no hesitation in affirming. We believe that this book will, to a great extent, supersede the manuals now used in our Catholic schools, and make its way by its own merits into Protestant places of education."—*Tablet.*

History of England. 58 B.C.—A.D. 1714. By H. F. WRIGHT, M.A., LL.D. New Edition, revised. Crown 8vo. 5*s*. net.

LONDON: G. BELL AND SONS, LTD.

A
SELECTED CATALOGUE

OF

EDUCATIONAL WORKS

PUBLISHED BY

G. BELL AND SONS, Ltd.

CONTENTS

LONDON: YORK HOUSE, PORTUGAL STREET, W.C.
CAMBRIDGE: DEIGHTON, BELL & CO.
NEW YORK: THE MACMILLAN COMPANY
BOMBAY: A. H. WHEELER & CO.

LATIN AND GREEK

Full Catalogue of Classical Books sent on application

Bell's Simplified Latin Texts

Edited, with Notes, Exercises, and Vocabulary, by S. E. WINBOLT, M.A., Christ's Hospital, Horsham. Crown 8vo. With numerous Illustrations. 1s. 6d. each.

FIRST LIST OF VOLUMES, NOW READY

Cæsar's Invasion of Britain.
Livy's Kings of Rome.
Vergil's Taking of Troy.
Vergil's Athletic Sports.

Simple Selections from Cicero's Letters.
Cæsar's Fifth Campaign (from De Bello Gallico, Book V.).

Bell's Illustrated Classics

Edited by E. C. MARCHANT, M.A.

Edited with Introductions, Notes and Vocabularies. Pott 8vo. With numerous illustrations, maps and plans, 1s. 6d. each ; except the GREEK PLAYS, which are 2s. each.

Cæsar. Book I. By A. C. LIDDELL, M.A.
—— Book II. By A. C. LIDDELL, M.A.
—— Book III. By F. H. COLSON, M.A., and G. M. GWYTHER, M.A.
—— Book IV. By Rev. A. W. UPCOTT, D.D.
—— Book V. By A. REYNOLDS, M.A.
—— Books IV. and V., in one volume, 2s. 6d.
—— Book VI. By J. T. PHILLIPSON, M.A.
—— Books V. and VI., in one volume, 2s. 6d.
—— Book VII. By S. E. WINBOLT, M.A.
Cæsar's Invasions of Britain (De Bello Gallico. Lib. IV. XX.—V. XXIII.). By Rev. A. W. UPCOTT, D.D., and A. REYNOLDS, M.A.
Cicero. Speeches against Catiline. I. and II. (1 vol.). By F. HERRING, M.A.
—— Selections. By J. F. CHARLES, B.A.
—— De Amicitia. By H. J. L. J. MASSÉ, M.A.
—— De Senectute. By A. S. WARMAN, B.A.
Cornelius Nepos. Epaminondas, Hannibal, Cato. By H. L. EARL, M.A.
Eutropius. Books I. and II. (1 vol.). By J. G. SPENCER, B.A.
Homer: Iliad. Book I. By L. D. WAINWRIGHT, M.A.
Horace: Odes. Book I. By C. G. BOTTING, B.A.
—— Book II. By C. G. BOTTING, B.A.
—— Book III. By H. LATTER, M.A.
—— Book IV. By H. LATTER, M.A.
Livy. Book IX., cc. i-xix. By W. C. FLAMSTEAD WALTERS, M.A.

Livy. Hannibal's First Campaign in Italy. (Selected from Book XXI.) By F. E. A. TRAVES, M.A.
Lucian: Vera Historia. By R. E. YATES, B.A.
Ovid: Metamorphoses. Book I. By G. H. WELLS, M.A.
—— Selection from the Metamorphoses. By J. W. E. PEARCE, M.A.
—— Elegiac Selections. By F. COVERLEY SMITH, B.A.
—— Tristia. Book I. By A. E. ROGERS, M.A.
—— Tristia. Book III. By H. R. WOOLRYCH, M.A.
Phaedrus: A Selection. By Rev. R. H. CHAMBERS, M.A.
Stories of Great Men. By Rev. F. CONWAY, M.A.
Virgil: Aeneid. Book I. By Rev. E. H. S. ESCOTT, M.A.
—— Book II. By L. D. WAINWRIGHT, M.A.
—— Book III. By L. D. WAINWRIGHT, M.A.
—— Book IV. By A. S. WARMAN, B.A.
—— Book V. By J. T. PHILLIPSON, M.A.
—— Book VI. By J. T. PHILLIPSON, M.A.
—— Books VII., VIII., IX., X., XI., XII. By L. D. WAINWRIGHT, M.A. 6 vols.
—— Selection from Books VII. to XII. By W. G. COAST, B.A.
—— Georgics. Book IV. By L. D. WAINWRIGHT, M.A.
Xenophon: Anabasis. Books I., II., III. By E. C. MARCHANT, M.A. 3 vols.

GREEK PLAYS (2s. *each*)

Aeschylus: Prometheus Vinctus. By C. E. LAURENCE, M.A.
Euripides: Alcestis. By E. H. BLAKENEY, M.A.

Euripides: Bacchae. By G. M. GWYTHER, M.A.
—— Hecuba. By Rev. A. W. UPCOTT, M.A.
—— Medea. By Rev. T. NICKLIN, M.A.

Bell's Illustrated Classics—Intermediate Series

Edited for higher forms, without Vocabularies. Crown 8vo. With Illustrations and Maps

Cæsar: Seventh Campaign in Gaul, B.C. 52. De Bello Gallico. Lib. VII. Edited by the Rev. W. COOKWORTHY COMPTON, M.A. 2s. 6d. net.
—— De Bello Civili. Book I. Edited by the Rev. W. J. BENSLEY, M.A. 2s. 6d. net.
Livy. Book XXI. Edited by F. E. A. TRAYES, M.A. 2s. 6d. net.
Tacitus: Agricola. Edited by J. W. E. PEARCE, M.A. 2s.

Sophocles: Antigone. Edited by G. H. WELLS, M.A. 2s. 6d. ret.

Homer: Odyssey. Book I. Edited by E. C. MARCHANT, M.A. 2s.

The Athenians in Sicily. Being portions of Thucydides, Books VI. and VII. Edited by the Rev. W. COOKWORTHY COMPTON, M.A. 2s. 6d. net.

Public School Series of Classical Authors

Edited with Introductions and Notes

Aristophanes. By F. A. PALE., M.A., LL.D. The Peace, 2s. 6d. The Acharnians, 2s. 6d. The Frogs, 2s. 6d.
Cicero: Letters of Cicero to Atticus. Book I. By A. PRETOR, M.A. 2s. 6d. net.
Demosthenes: De Falsa Legatione. By the late R. SHILLETO, M.A. 6s.
Livy. Book VI. By E. S. WEYMOUTH, M.A., and G. F. HAMILTON B.A. 2s. 6d.
Plato: Protagoras. By W. WAYTE, M.A. 4s. 6d.
—— Apology of Socrates and Cito. By W. WAGNER, PH.D. 2s. 6d.
—— Phaedo. By W. WAGNER, PH.D. 5s. 6d.

Plato: Gorgias. By W. H. THOMPSON, D.D 6s.
—— Republic. Books I. and II. By G. H. WELLS, M.A. 5s.
Plautus. By WILHELM WAGNER, PH.D. Menaechmei, 4s. 6d. Trinummus, 4s. 6d. Aulularia, 4s. 6d.
Sophocles: Trachiniæ. By A. PRETOR, M.A. 2s. 6d.
—— Œdipus Tyrannus. By B. H. KENNEDY, D.D. 2s. 6d.
Terence. By W. WAGNER, PH.D. 7s. 6d.
Thucydides. Book VI. By T. H. DOUGAN, M.A. 2s.

Grammar School Classics

Edited with Introductions and Notes

Catullus, Tibullus, and Propertius. Selected Poems. By the Rev. A. H. WRATIS-LAW and F. N. SUTTON, B.A. 2s. 6d.
Horace. By A. J. MACLEANE, M.A. 3s. 6d. Or, Part I., Odes, 2s.; Part II., Satires and Epistles, 2s.
Juvenal. Sixteen Satires (expurgated). By HERMAN PRIOR, M.A. 3s. 6d.
Martial. Select Epigrams. By F. A. PALEY, M.A., LL.D., and the late W. H. STONE, 4s. 6d.
Ovid: Fasti. By F. A. PALEY, M.A., LL.D. Books III. and IV. 1s. 6d.

Sallust: Catilina and Jugurtha. By G. LONG, M.A., and J. G. FRAZER, M.A. 3s. 6d. Or separately, 2s. each.
Virgil: Conington's Edition, abridged. Bucolics, Georgics, and Aeneid. Books I.–IV., 4s. 6d. Aeneid. Books V.–XII., 4s. 6d. Or in 9 separate parts, 1s. 6d. each.
Xenophon: Anabasis. With Life, Itinerary, Index, and Three Maps. By J. F. MACMICHAEL. In 4 volumes, 1s. 6d. each.
—— Cyropaedia. By G. M. GORHAM, M.A., 3s. 6d. Books I. and II., 1s. 6d. Books V. and VI., 1s. 6d.
—— Memorabilia. By P. FROST, M.A. 3s.

Cambridge Texts with Notes

Price 1*s.* 6*d.* each, with exceptions

Aeschylus. 6 Vols. Prometheus Vinctus —Septem contra Thebas—Agamemnon—Persae—Eumenides—Choephoroe. By F. A. PALEY, M.A., LL.D.

Cicero. 3 Vols. De Amicitia—De Senectute —Epistolae Selectae. By GEORGE LONG, M.A.

Euripides. 11 Vols. Alcestis—Hippolytus —Hecuba—Bacchae—Ion (2*s.*)—Phoenissae —Troades—Hercules Furens—Andromache —Iphigenia in Tauris—Supplices. By F. A. PALEY, M.A., LL.D.

Ovid. Selections from the Amores, Tristia, Heroides, and Metamorphoses. By A. J. MACLEANE, M.A.

Ovid. Fasti. Books III. and IV.—Books V. and VI. By F. A. PALEY, LL.D. 2*s.* each.

Sophocles. 4 Vols. Oedipus Tyrannus—Antigone—Electra—Ajax. By F. A. PALEY, M.A., LL.D.

Terence. 4 Vols. Andria—Hautontimorumenos — Phormio — Adelphi. By Prof. WAGNER.

Virgil. 12 Vols. Abridged from Prof. CONINGTON'S Edition by Professors NETTLESHIP and WAGNER and Rev. J. G. SHEPPARD.

Xenophon: Anabasis. 6 Vols. MACMICHAEL'S Edition, revised by J. E. MELHUISH, M.A. In separate Books.
Book I.—Books II. and III.—Book IV.—Book V.—Book VI.—Book VII.

Xenophon: Hellenica. Book I. and Book II. By the Rev. L. D. DOWDALL, M.A., B.D. 2*s.* each.

Cambridge Texts

Aeschylus. By F. A. PALEY, M.A., LL.D. 2*s.*

Caesar De Bello Gallico. By G. LONG, M.A. 1*s.* 6*d.*

Ciceronis Orationes in Verrem. By G. LONG, M.A. 2*s.* 6*d.*

Euripides. By F. A. PALEY, M.A., LL.D. 3 vols. 2*s.* each.

Herodotus. By J. W. BLAKESLEY, B.D. 2 vols. 2*s.* 6*d* each.

Horatius. By A. J. MACLEANE, M.A. 1*s.* 6*d.*

Juvenalis et Persius. By A. J. MACLEANE, M.A. 1*s.* 6*d.*

Lucretius. By H. A. J. MUNRO, M.A. 2*s.*

Ovidius. By A. PALMER, M.A., G. M. EDWARDS, M.A., G. A. DAVIES, M.A., S. G. OWEN, M.A., A. E. HOUSMAN, M.A., and J. P. POSTGATE, M.A., LITT.D. 3 vols. 2*s.* each.

Sallusti Catalina et Jugurtha. By G. LONG, M.A. 1*s.* 6*d.*

Sophocles. By F. A. PALEY, M.A., LL.D. 2*s.* 6*d.*

Terentius. By W. WAGNER, PH.D. 2*s.*

Thucydides. By J. W. DONALDSON, B.D. 2 vols. 2*s.* each.

Vergilius. By J. CONINGTON, M.A. 2*s.*

Xenophontis Anabasis. By J. F. MACMICHAEL. M.A. 1*s.* 6*d.*

Novum Testamentum Graece. Edited by F. H. SCRIVENER, M.A. 4*s.* 6*d.*
—— Editio Major. Containing the readings approved by Bp. Westcott and Dr. Hort, and those adopted by the revisers, etc. Small post 8vo. New Edition, with emendations and corrections by Prof. EB. NESTLE. Printed on India paper, limp cloth, 6*s.* net; limp leather, 7*s.* 6*d.* net; or interleaved with writing paper, limp leather, 10*s.* 6*d.* net.

Other Editions, Texts, &c.

Anthologia Latina. A Selection of Choice Latin Poetry, with Notes. By Rev. F. ST. JOHN THACKERAY, M.A. 16mo. 4*s.* 6*d.*

Anthologia Graeca. A Selection from the Greek Poets. By Rev. F. ST. JOHN THACKERAY, M.A. 16mo. 4*s.* 6*d.*

Aristophanis Comoediae. Edited by H. A. HOLDEN, LL.D. Demy 8vo. 18*s.*
The Plays separately: Acharnenses, 2*s.*; Equites, 1*s.* 6*d.*; Nubes, 2*s.*; Vespae, 2*s.*; Pax, 2*s.*; Lysistrata, et Thesmophoriazusae, 4*s.*; Aves, 2*s.*; Ranae, 2*s.*; Plutus, 2*s.*

Aristophanes, The Comedies of. The Greek Text, revised, and a Metrical Translation on Opposite Pages, together with Introduction and Commentary. By BENJAMIN BICKLEY ROGERS, M.A. 6 vols. Fcap. 4to. 15*s.* each.
Now Ready: Vol. I., containing The

Acharnians and the Knights; Vol. IV., containing The Lysistrata and The These mophoriazusae; and Vol. V., containing The Frogs and The Ecclesiazusae; and the following separate plays: Acharnians, 10*s.* 6*d.*; Knights, 10*s.* 6*d.*; Frogs, 10*s.* 6*d.*; Ecclesiazusae, 7*s.* 6*d.*; Lysistrata, 10*s.* 6*d.*; Thesmophoriazusae, 7*s.* 6*d.*; Birds, 10*s.* 6*d.*; Plutus (with the Menæchmi of Plautus), 8*s.* 6*d.*; Menæchmi, separately, 1*s.* 6*d.*

Catullus. Edited by J. P. POSTGATE. M.A., LITT.D. Fcap. 8vo. 3*s.*

Corpus Poetarum Latinorum, a se aliisque denuo recognitorum et brevi lectionum varietate instructorum, edidit JOHANNES PERCIVAL POSTGATE, LITT.D. 2 vols. Large post 4to. 25*s.* net each. Or in Five Parts. Parts I. and II., 12*s.* net each; Parts III. and IV., 9*s.* net each; Part V., 6*s.* net.

Other Editions, Texts, &c.—*continued*

Corpus Poetarum Latinorum. Edited by WALKER. 1 thick vol. 8vo. Cloth, 18*s.*

Hall. Mundus Alter et Idem. Edited as a School Reader by H. J. ANDERSON, M.A. 2*s.*

Horace. The Latin Text, with Conington's Translation on opposite pages. Pocket Edition. 4*s.* net; or in leather, 5*s.* net. Also in 2 vols., limp leather. The Odes, 2*s.* net; Satires and Epistles, 2*s. 6d.* net.

Livy. The first five Books. PRENDEVILLE'S edition revised by J. H. FREESE, M.A. Books I., II., III., IV., V. 1*s. 6d.* each.

Lucan. The Pharsalia. By C. E. HASKINS, M.A. With an Introduction by W. E. HEITLAND, M.A. Demy 8vo. 14*s.*

Lucretius. Titi Lucreti Cari de rerum natura libri sex. Edited with Notes, Introduction, and Translation, by the late H. A. J. MUNRO. 3 vols. 8vo. Vols. I. and II. Introduction, Text, and Notes, 18*s.* Vol. III. Translation, 6*s.*

Ovid. The Metamorphoses. Book XIII. With Introduction and Notes by Prof. C. H. KEENE, M A. 2*s. 6d.*

Ovid. The Metamorphoses. Book XIV. With Introduction and Notes by Prof. C. H. KEENE, M.A. 2*s. 6d.*
  ✱✱✱ Books XIII. and XIV. together. 3*s. 6d.*

Persius. A Persii Flacci Satirarum Liber. Edited, with Introduction and Notes by A. PRETOR, M.A. 3*s. 6d.* net.

Pindar. Myths from Pindar. Selected and edited by H. R. KING, M.A. With Illustrations. Post 8vo. 2*s. 6d.* net.

Plato. The Proem to the Republic of Plato. (Book I. and Book II. chaps. 1–10.) Edited, with Introduction, Critical Notes, and Commentary, by Prof. T. G. TUCKER, LITT.D. 6*s.*

Petronii Cena Trimalchionis. Edited and Translated by W. D. LOWE, M.A. 7*s. 6d.* net.

Propertius. Sexti Properti Carmina recognovit J. P. POSTGATE, LITT.D. 4to. 3*s.* net.

Rutilius: Rutilii Claudii Namatiani de Reditu Suo Libri Duo. With Introduction and Notes by Prof. C. H. KEENE, M.A., and English Verse Translation by G. F. SAVAGE ARMSTRONG, M.A. 7*s. 6d.* net.

Theocritus. Edited, with Introduction and Notes, by R. J. CHOLMELEY, M.A. Crown 8vo. 7*s. 6d.*

Theognis. The Elegies of Theognis, and other Elegies included in the Theognidean Sylloge. With Introduction, Commentary, and Appendices, by J. HUDSON WILLIAMS, M.A. Crown 8vo. 7*s. 6d.* net.

Thucydides. The History of the Peloponnesian War. With Notes and a Collation of the MSS. By the late R. SHILLETO, M.A. Book I. 8vo, 6*s. 6d,* Book II. 5*s. 6d.*

Latin and Greek Class Books

Bell's Illustrated Latin Readers. Edited by E. C. MARCHANT, M.A. Pott 8vo. With brief Notes, Vocabularies, and numerous Illustrations. 1*s.* each.

Scalae Primae. A Selection of Simple Stories for Translation into English.

Scalae Mediae. Short Extracts from Eutropius and Caesar.

Scalae Tertiae. Selections in Prose and Verse from Phaedrus, Ovid, Nepos and Cicero.

Latin Picture Cards. Edited by Prof. FRANK S. GRANGER, M.A. Sixteen cards printed in colours, with Vocabularies and Exercises. 1*s. 3d.* net.

Bell's Illustrated Latin Course, for the First Year. In three Parts. By E. C. MARCHANT, M.A., and J. G. SPENCER, B.A. With numerous Illustrations. 1*s* 6*d.* each.

Bell's Concise Latin Course. Part I. By E. C. MARCHANT, M.A., and J. G. SPENCER, B.A. 2*s.*

Bell's Concise Latin Course. Part II. By E. C. MARCHANT, M.A., and S. E. WINBOLT, M.A. 2*s. 6d.*

Cothurnulus. Three Short Latin Historical Plays. By Prof. E. V. ARNOLD, LITT.D. With or without Vocabulary, 1*s.* Vocabulary separately, 4*d.*

Easy Latin Plays. By M. L. NEWMAN. 6*d.*

Eclogæ Latinæ; or, First Latin Reading Book. With Notes and Vocabulary by the late Rev. P. FROST, M.A. 1*s. 6d.*

Latin Exercises and Grammar Papers. By T. COLLINS, M.A. 2*s. 6d.*

Unseen Papers in Latin Prose and Verse. By T. COLLINS, M.A. 2*s. 6d.*

Latin Unseens. Selected and arranged by E. C. MARCHANT, M.A. 1*s.*

Latin Reader (Verse and Prose). By W KING GILLIES, M.A., and H. J. ANDERSON, M.A. 2*s.*

Latin of the Empire (Prose and Verses). By W. KING GILLIES, M.A., and A. R. CUMMING, M.A. 4*s. 6d.*

First Exercises in Latin Prose Composition. By E. A. WELLS, M.A. With Vocabulary. 1*s.*

Materials for Latin Prose Composition. By the Rev. P. FROST, M.A. 2*s.* Key, 4*s.* net.

Passages for Translation into Latin Prose. By Prof. H. NETTLESHIP, M.A. 3*s.* Key, 4*s.* net.

Easy Translations from Nepos, Cæsar, Cicero, Livy, &c., for Retranslation into Latin. By T. COLLINS, M.A. 2*s.*

Latin and Greek Class Books—*continued*

Memorabilia Latina. By F. W. LEVANDER, F.R.A.S. 1*s.*

Test Questions on the Latin Language. By F. W. LEVANDER, F.R.A.S. 1*s.* 6*d.*

Latin Syntax Exercises. By L. D. WAINWRIGHT, M.A. Five Parts. 8*d.* each.

A Latin Verse Book. By the Rev. P. FROST, M.A. 2*s.* Key, 5*s.* net.

Latin Elegiac Verse, Easy Exercises in. By the Rev. J. PENROSE. 2*s.* Key, 3*s.* 6*d.* net.

Foliorum Silvula. Part I. Passages for Translation into Latin Elegiac and Heroic Verse. By H. A. HOLDEN, LL.D. 7*s.* 6*d.*

How to Pronounce Latin. By J. P. POSTGATE, LITT.D. 1*s.* net.

Res Romanae, being brief Aids to the History, Geography, Literature and Antiquities of Ancient Rome. By E. P. COLERIDGE, M.A. With 3 maps. 2*s.* 6*d.*

Climax Prote. A First Greek Reader, With Hints and Vocabulary. By E. C. MARCHANT, M.A. With 30 illustrations. 1*s.* 6*d.*

Greek Verbs. By J. S. BAIRD, T.C.D. 2*s.* 6*d.*

Analecta Græca Minora. With Notes and Dictionary. By the Rev. P. FROST, M.A. 2*s.*

Unseen Papers in Greek Prose and Verse. By T. COLLINS, M.A. 3*s.*

Notes on Greek Accents. By the Rt. Rev. A. BARRY, D.D. 1*s.*

Res Graecae. Being Aids to the study of the History, Geography, Archæology, and Literature of Ancient Athens. By E. P. COLERIDGE, M.A. With 5 Maps, 7 Plans, and 17 other illustrations. 5*s.*

Notabilia Quaedam. 1*s.*

Bell's Classical Translations
Crown 8vo.   Paper Covers.   1*s.* each

Æschylus: Translated by WALTER HEADLAM, LITT.D., and C. E. S. HEADLAM, M.A. Agamemnon—The Suppliants—Choephoroe—Eumenides — Prometheus Bound — Persians—Seven against Thebes.

Aristophanes: The Acharnians. Translated by W. H. COVINGTON, B.A.
—— The Plutus. Translated by M. T. QUINN, M.A.

Cæsar's Gallic War. Translated by W. A. M'DEVITTE, B.A. 2 Vols. (Books I.-IV., and Books V.-VII.).

Cicero: Friendship and Old Age. Translated by G. H. WELLS, M.A.
—— Orations. Translated by Prof. C. D. YONGE, M.A. 6 vols. Catiline, Murena, Sulla and Archias (in one vol.), Manilian Law, Sextius, Milo.

Demosthenes on the Crown. Translated by C. RANN KENNEDY.

Euripides. Translated by E. P. COLERIDGE, M.A. 14 vols. Medea—Alcestis—Heracleidæ—Hippolytus — Supplices—Troades—Ion —Andromache — Bacchæ — Hecuba — Hercules Furens—Orestes—Iphigenia in Tauris.

Homer's Iliad, Books I. and II., Books III.-IV., Books V.-VI., Books VII.-VIII., Books IX.-X., Books XI.-XII., Books XIII.-XIV., Books XV. and XVI. Translated by E. H. BLAKENEY, M.A. 8 vols.
—— Book XXIV. Translated by E. H. BLAKENEY, M.A.

Horace. Translated by A. HAMILTON BRYCE, LL.D. 4 vols. Odes, Books I. and II.—Odes, Books III. and IV., Carmen Seculare and Epodes—Satires—Epistles and Ars Poetica.

Livy. Books I., II., III., IV. Translated by J. H. FREESE, M.A. With Maps. 4 vols.
—— Books V. and VI. Translated by E. S. WEYMOUTH, M.A. Lond. With Maps. 2 vols.
—— Book IX. Translated by FRANCIS STORR, M.A. With Map.
—— Books XXI., XXII., XXIII. Translated by J. BERNARD BAKER, M.A. 3 vols.

Lucan: The Pharsalia. Book I. Translated by FREDERICK CONWAY, M.A.

Ovid's Fasti. Translated by HENRY T. RILEY, M.A. 3 vols. Books I. and II.—Books III. and IV.—Books V. and VI.
—— Tristia. Translated by HENRY T. RILEY, M.A.

Plato: Apology of Socrates and Crito (1 vol.), Phædo, and Protagoras. Translated by H. CARY, M.A. 3 vols.

Plautus: Trinummus. Aulularia, Menæchmi, and Captivi. Translated by HENRY T. RILEY, M.A. 4 vols.

Sophocles. Translated by E. P. COLERIDGE, M.A. 7 vols. Antigone—Philoctetes—Œdipus Rex—Œdipus Coloneus—Electra—Trachiniæ—Ajax.

Thucydides. Book VI. Translated by E. C. MARCHANT, M.A.
—— Book VII. Translated by E. C. MARCHANT, M.A.

Virgil, Translated by A. HAMILTON BRYCE, LL.D. 6 vols. Bucolics — Georgics — Æneid, 1-3—Æneid, 4-6—Æneid, 7-9— Æneid, 10-12.

Xenophon's Anabasis. Translated by the Rev. J. S. WATSON, M.A. With Map. 3 vols. Books I. and II.—Books III., IV., and V.—Books VI. and VII.
—— Hellenics. Books I. and II. Translated by the Rev. H. DALE, M.A.

*** *For other Translations from the Classics, see the Catalogue of Bohn's Libraries, which will be forwarded on application*

MATHEMATICS

Full Catalogue of Mathematical Books post free on application

Cambridge Mathematical Series

Public School Arithmetic. By W. M. BAKER, M.A., and A. A. BOURNE, M.A. 3s. 6d. Or with Answers 4s 6d.

The Student's Arithmetic. By W. M. BAKER, M A., and A. A. BOURNE, M A. With or without Answers. 2s 6d.

New School Arithmetic. By C. PENDLEBURY, M.A., and F. E. ROBINSON, M.A. With or without Answers. 4s. 6d. In Two Parts. 2s. 6d. each.
   Key to Part II., 8s. 6d. net.

New School Examples in a separate volume, 3s. Or in Two Parts, 1s. 6d. and 2s.

Arithmetic, with 8000 Examples. By C. PENDLEBURY, M.A. 4s. 6d. In Two Parts. 2s. 6d. each.
   Key to Part II., 7s. 6d. net.

Examples in Arithmetic. Extracted from the above. 3s. Or in Two Parts 1s. 6d. and 2s.

Commercial Arithmetic. By C. PENDLEBURY, M.A., and W. S. BEARD, F.R.G.S. 2s. 6d. Part I. separately, 1s. Part II., 1s. 6d.

Arithmetic for Indian Schools. By C. PENDLEBURY, M.A., and T. S. TAIT. 3s.

Examples in Arithmetic By C. O. TUCKEY, M.A. With or without Answers. 3s.

Junior Practical Mathematics. By W. J. STAINER, B.A. 2s., with Answers, 2s. 6d. Part I., 1s. 4d., with Answers, 1s. 6d. Part II., 1s. 4d.

Elementary Algebra. By W. M. BAKER, M.A., and A. A. BOURNE, M.A. With or without Answers. 4s. 6d. In Two Parts. Part I., 2s. 6d., or with Answers, 3s. Part II., with or without Answers, 2s. 6d.
   Key, 10s. net ; or in 2 Parts, 5s. net each.

Examples in Algebra. Extracted from above. With or without Answers, 3s. Or in Two Parts. Part I., 1s. 6d., or with Answers, 2s. Part II., with or without Answers, 2s.

Examples in Algebra. By C. O. TUCKEY, M A. With or without Answers. 3s.
   — **Supplementary Examples.** 6d. net.

Elementary Algebra for use in Indian Schools. By J. T. HATHORNTHWAITE, M.A. 2s.

Choice and Chance. By W. A. WHITWORTH, M.A. 7s. 6d.
   — **DCC Exercises,** including Hints for the Solution of all the Questions in "Choice and Chance." 6s.

Euclid Books I.—VI., and part of Book XI. By HORACE DEIGHTON, M.A. 4s. 6d., or in separate books.

Introduction to Euclid. By HORACE DEIGHTON, M.A., and O. EMTAGE, B.A. 1s. 6d.

Euclid. Exercises on Euclid and in Modern Geometry. By J. McDOWELL, M.A. 6s.

Elementary Graphs. By W. M. BAKER, M.A., and A. A. BOURNE, M.A. 6d. net.

A New Geometry. By W. M. BAKER, M.A. and A. A. BOURNE, M.A. Crown 8vo. 2s. 6d. Also Books I.-III. separately, 1s. 6d.

Elementary Geometry. By W. M. BAKER, M.A., and A. A. BOURNE, M.A. 4s. 6d. Or in Parts. *Full list on request.*
   Answers to Examples, 6d. net. Key, 6s. net.

Geometry for Schools. By W. G. BORCHARDT, M.A., and the Rev. A. D. PERROTT, M A. Vol. I., 1s. ; Vol. II., 1s. 6d. ; Vol. III., 1s. ; Vols. I.-III., 2s. 6d. ; Vol. IV., 1s. ; Vols. I.-IV., 3s. 6d.
   [Vols. V. and VI., *in the Press.*

Examples in Practical Geometry and Mensuration. By J. W. MARSHALL, M.A., and C. O. TUCKEY, M.A. 1s. 6d.

A New Trigonometry for Schools. By W. G. BORCHARDT, M.A., and the Rev. A. D PERROTT, M.A. 4s. 6d. Or in Two Parts, 2s. 6d. each.
   Key, 10s. net ; or in 2 Parts, 5s. net each.

Elementary Trigonometry. By CHARLES PENDLEBURY, M.A., F.R.A.S. 4s. 6d.

Short Course of Elementary Plane Trigonometry. By CHARLES PENDLEBURY, M.A. 2s. 6d.

Elementary Trigonometry. By J. M. DYER, M.A., and the Rev. R. H. WHITCOMBE, M.A. 4s. 6d.

Algebraic Geometry. By W. M. BAKER, M.A. 6s. Part I. (The Straight Line and Circle), 2s. 6d. Key, 7s. 6d. net.

Practical Solid Geometry. By the Rev. PERCY UNWIN, M.A. 3s. 6d.

Analytical Geometry for Beginners. By Rev. T. G. VYVYAN, M.A. Part I. The Straight Line and Circle. 2s. 6d.

Conic Sections, treated Geometrically. By W. H. BESANT, Sc.D., F.R.S. 4s. 6d. Key, 5s. net.

Elementary Conics, being the first 8 chapters of the above. 2s. 6d.

Conics, the Elementary Geometry of. By Rev. C. TAYLOR, D.D. 5s.

Calculus for Beginners. By W. M. BAKER, M.A. 3s.

Differential Calculus for Beginners. By A. LODGE, M.A. With Introduction by Sir OLIVER LODGE. 4s. 6d.

Integral Calculus for Beginners. By A. LODGE, M.A. 4s. 6d.

Roulettes and Glissettes. By W. H. BESANT, Sc.D., F.R.S. 5s.

Geometrical Optics. An Elementary Treatise by W. S. ALDIS, M.A. 4s.

Practical Mathematics. By H. A. STERN, M.A., and W. H. TOPHAM. 6s. ; or Part I., 2s. 6d. ; Part II., 3s. 6d.

Elementary Hydrostatics. By W. H. BESANT, Sc.D. 4s. 6d. Solutions, 5s. net.

Elements of Hydrostatics. By C. M. JESSOP, M.A., and G. W. CAUNT, M.A. 2s. 6d.

Cambridge Mathematical Series—*continued*

Elementary Mechanics. By C. M. JESSOP, M.A., and J. H. HAVELOCK, M.A., D.Sc. 4s. 6d.

Experimental Mechanics for Schools. By FRED CHARLES, M.A., and W. H. HEWITT, B.A., B.Sc. 3s. 6d.

The Student's Dynamics. Comprising Statics and Kinetics. By G. M. MINCHIN, M.A.; F.R.S. 3s. 6d.

Elementary Dynamics. By W. M. BAKER, M.A. New Revised Edition, 4s. 6d. Key, 10s. 6d. net.

Elementary Dynamics. By W. GARNETT, M.A., D.C.L. 6s.

Dynamics, A Treatise on. By W. H. BESANT, Sc.D., F.R.S. 10s. 6d.

Heat, An Elementary Treatise on. By W. GARNETT, M.A., D.C.L. 4s. 6d.

Elementary Physics, Examples and Examination Papers in. By W. GALLATLY, M.A. 4s.

Mechanics, A Collection of Problems in Elementary. By W. WALTON, M.A. 6s.

Uniform Volume

Geometrical Drawing. For Army and other Examinations. By R. HARRIS. 3s. 6d.

The Junior Cambridge Mathematical Series.

A Junior Arithmetic. By C. PENDLEBURY, M.A., and F. E. ROBINSON, M.A. 1s. 6d. With Answers, 2s.

Examples from a Junior Arithmetic. Extracted from the above. 1s. With Answers, 1s. 6d.

A First Algebra. By W. M. BAKER, M.A., and A. A. BOURNE, M.A. 1s. 6d.; or with Answers, 2s.

A First Geometry. By W. M. BAKER, M.A., and A. A. BOURNE, M.A. With or without Answers. 1s. 6d.

Elementary Mensuration. By W. M. BAKER, M.A., and A.A. BOURNE, M.A. 1s. 6d.

Other Mathematical Works

The Mathematical Gazette. Edited by W. J. GREENSTREET, M.A. (Jan., March, May, July, Oct. and Dec.) 1s. 6d. net.

The Teaching of Elementary Mathematics, being the Reports of the Committee of the Mathematical Association. 6d. net.

The Teaching of Mathematics in Preparatory Schools. Report of the Mathl. Assn. Committee, Nov., 1907. 3d. net.

The Teaching of Elementary Algebra and Numerical Trigonometry. Being the Report of the Mathl. Assoc. Committee, 1911. 3d. net.

The Correlation of Mathematics and Science. Report of the Mathl. Assn. Committee. 6d. net.

A New Shilling Arithmetic. By C. PENDLEBURY, M.A., and F. E. ROBINSON, M.A. 1s.; or with Answers, 1s. 4d.

A Shilling Arithmetic. By CHARLES PENDLEBURY, M.A., and W. S. BEARD, F.R.G.S. 1s. With Answers, 1s. 4d.

Elementary Arithmetic. By the same Authors. 1s. 6d. With or without Answers.

Graduated Arithmetic, for Junior and Private Schools. By the same Authors. Parts I., II., and III., 3d. each; Parts IV., V., and VI., 4d. each; Part VII., 6d. Answers to Parts I. and II., 4d. net; Parts III.-VII., 4d. net each.

Arithmetic for the Standards (Scheme B). Standard I., sewed, 2d., cloth, 3d.; II., III., IV., and V., sewed, 3d. each, cloth, 4d. each; VI. and VII., sewed, 4d. each, cloth, 6d. each. Answers to each Standard, 4d. net each.

Exercises and Examination Papers in Arithmetic, Logarithms and Mensuration. By C. PENDLEBURY, M.A. 2s. 6d. New Edition. Key, 5s. net. [*In the Press.*

Test Cards in Arithmetic (Scheme B). By C. PENDLEBURY, M.A. For Standards II., III., IV., V., VI. and VII. 1s. net each.

Public School Examination Papers in Mathematics. Compiled by P. A. OPENSHAW, B.A. 1s. 6d.

Bell's New Practical Arithmetic. By W. J. STAINER, M.A. 1st, 2nd, 3rd, 4th, 5th and 6th Years, paper, 3d. each, cloth, 4d. each; 7th Year, paper, 4d., cloth, 6d. Teachers' Books, 8d. net each Year.

Bell's New Practical Arithmetic Test Cards, for the 2nd, 3rd, 4th, 5th, 6th, and 7th years. 1s. 3d. net each.

Graduated Exercises in Addition (Simple and Compound). By W. S. BEARD. 1s.

Algebra for Elementary Schools. By W. M. BAKER, M.A., and A. A. BOURNE, M.A. Three stages, 6d. each. Cloth, 8d. each. Answers, 4s. net each.

A First Year's Course in Geometry and Physics. By ERNEST YOUNG, B.Sc. 2s. 6d. Parts I. and II. 1s. 6d.; or Part III. 1s.

Trigonometry, Examination Papers in. By G. H. WARD, M.A. 2s. 6d. Key, 5s. net.

Euclid, The Elements of. The Enunciations and Figures. By the late J. BRASSE, D.D. 1s. Without the Figures, 6d.

Hydromechanics. By W. H. BESANT, Sc.D., and A. S. RAMSEY, M.A. Part I., Hydrostatics. 6s.

Hydrodynamics and Sound, An Elementary Treatise on. By A. B. BASSET, M.A., F.R.S. 8s.

The Geometry of Surfaces. By A. B. BASSET, M.A., F.R.S. 10s. 6d.

Elementary Treatise on Cubic and Quartic Curves. By A. B. BASSET, M.A., F.R.S. 10s. 6d.

Analytical Geometry. By Rev. T. G. VYVYAN, M.A. 4s. 6d.

Book-keeping

Book-keeping by Double Entry, Theoretical, Practical, and for Examination Purposes. By J. T. MEDHURST, A.K.C., F.S.S. 1s. 6d.

Book-keeping, Examination Papers in. Compiled by JOHN T. MEDHURST, A.K.C., F.S S. 3s. Key, 2s. 6d. net.

Book-keeping, Graduated Exercises and Examination Papers in. Compiled by P. MURRAY. F.S.S.S., F.Sc S. (Lond.). 2s. 6d.

Text Book of the Principles and Practice of Book-keeping and Estate-Office Work. By Prof. A. W. THOMSON, B.Sc. 5s.

ENGLISH

Mason's New English Grammars. Revised by A. J. ASHTON, M.A.
A Junior English Grammar. 1s.
Intermediate English Grammar. 2s.
Senior English Grammar. 3s. 6d.

GRAMMARS

By C. P. MASON B.A., F.C.P.

First Notions of Grammar for Young Learners. 1s.

First Steps in English Grammar, for Junior Classes. 1s.

Outlines of English Grammar, for the Use of Junior Classes. 2s.

English Grammar; including the principles of Grammatical Analysis. 3s. 6d.

A Shorter English Grammar. 3s. 6d.

Practice and Help in the Analysis of Sentences. 2s.

English Grammar Practice. 1s.

Elementary English Grammar through Composition. By J. D. ROSE, M.A. 1s.

Advanced English Grammar through Composition. By JOHN D. ROSE, M.A. 2s. 6d.

Preparatory English Grammar. By W. BENSON, M.A. New Edition. 1s. net.

Rudiments of English Grammar and Analysis. By ERNEST ADAMS, PH.D. 1s.

Examples for Analysis in Verse and Prose. Selected by F. EDWARDS. 1s.

The Paraphrase of Poetry. By EDMUND CANDLER. 1s.

Essays and Essay-Writing, for Public Examinations. By A. W. READY, B.A. 3s. 6d.

Précis and Précis-Writing. By A. W. READY, B.A. 3s. 6d. Or without Key, 2s. 6d.

Elements of the English Language. By ERNEST ADAMS, PH.D. Revised by J. F. DAVIS, M.A., D.LIT. 4s. 6d.

History of the English Language. By Prof. T. R. LOUNSBURY. 5s. net.

The Teaching of English Literature in the Secondary School. By R. S. BATE, M.A. 2s. 6d. [*Ready Autumn*, 1912

A Concise Primer of English Literature. By W. H. HUDSON. 2s. 6d. [*In the Press*

Ten Brink's Early English Literature. 3 vols. 3s. 6d. each.

Introduction to English Literature. By HENRY S. PANCOAST. 5s. net.

A First View of English Literature. By HENRY S. PANCOAST and PERCY VAN DYKE SHELLY. Crown 8vo. 5s. net.

Introduction to American Literature. By H. S. PANCOAST. 4s. 6d. net.

The Foreign Debt of English Literature. By T. G. TUCKER, LITT.D. Post 8vo. 6s. net.

Handbooks of English Literature. Edited by Prof. HALES. 3s. 6d. net each.
The Age of Alfred. (660-1154). By F. J. SNELL, M.A.
The Age of Chaucer. (1346-1400.) By F. J. SNELL, M.A.
The Age of Transition. (1400-1580.) By F. J. SNELL, M.A. 2 vols.
The Age of Shakespeare. (1579-1631.) By THOMAS SECCOMBE and J. W. ALLEN. 2 vols. Vol. I. Poetry and Prose. Vol. II. Drama.
The Age of Milton. (1632-1660.) By the Rev. J. H. B. MASTERMAN, M.A., with Introduction, etc., by J. BASS MULLINGER, M.A.
The Age of Dryden. (1660-1700.) By R. GARNETT, LL.D., C.B.
The Age of Pope. (1700-1744.) By JOHN DENNIS.
The Age of Johnson. (1744-1798.) By THOMAS SECCOMBE.
The Age of Wordsworth. (1798-1832.) By Prof. C. H. HERFORD, LITT.D.
The Age of Tennyson. (1830-1870.) By Prof. HUGH WALKER.

Notes on Shakespeare's Plays. By T. DUFF BARNETT, B.A. 1s. each.
Midsummer Night's Dream.—Julius Cæsar.—The Tempest.—Macbeth.—Henry V.—Hamlet. — Merchant of Venice. — King Richard II.—King John.—King Richard III.—King Lear.—Coriolanus. - Twelfth Night.—As You Like It.—Much Ado About Nothing.

Principles of English Verse. By C. M. LEWIS. 5s. net.

Introduction to Poetry. By RAYMOND M. ALDEN. 5s.

Matriculation Précis. By S. E. WINBOLT, M.A. 1s. net Or with Key, 1s. 6d. net.

General Intelligence Papers. With Exercises in English Composition. By G. BLUNT. 2s. 6d.

Bell's English Texts for Secondary Schools

Edited by A. Guthkelch, M.A.

Browning's The Pied Piper, and other Poems. Edited by A. Guthkelch. 8*d.*

Fairy Poetry. Selected and edited by R. S. Bate, M.A. 1*s.*

Hawthorne's Wonder Book and Tanglewood Tales. Selected and Edited by H. Hampshire, M.A. 1*s.*

Kingsley's Heroes. Edited by L. H. Pond, B.A. With 2 maps. 1*s.*

Lamb's Tales from Shakespeare. Selected and edited by R. S. Bate, M.A. 10*d.*

Lamb's Adventures of Ulysses. Selections. Edited by A. C. Dunstan, Ph.D. 8*d.*

Stories of King Arthur, from Malory and Tennyson. Edited by R. S. Bate, M.A. 1*s.*

The Story of Enid, from Tennyson and The Mabinogion. By H. A. Treble, M.A. 10*d.*

Scott's A Legend of Montrose. Abridged and edited by F. C. Luckhurst. 1*s.*

Charles Reade's The Cloister and the Hearth. Abridged and edited by the Rev. A. E. Hall, B.A. 1*s.*

Hakluyt's Voyages. A Selection edited by the Rev. A. E. Hall, B.A. 1*s.*

Coleridge's The Ancient Mariner; and Selected Old English Ballads. Edited by A. Guthkelch, M.A. 1*s.*

Selections from Boswell's Life of Johnson. Edited by E. A. J. Marsh. 1*s.*

Selections from Ruskin. Edited by H. Hampshire, M.A. 1*s.*

Lockhart's Life of Scott. Selections edited by A. Barter, LL.A. 1*s.*

Charles Lamb's Selected Essays and Letters. Edited by A. Guthkelch, M.A. With Map of London. 1*s.* 4*d.*

Selections from Carlyle. Edited by Elizabeth Lee. 1*s.*

English Odes. Edited by E. A. J. Marsh, M.A. 1*s.*

Bell's English Classics

Bacon's Essays. (Selected.) Edited by A. E. Roberts, M.A. 1*s.*

Browning Selections from. Edited by F. Ryland, M.A. 1*s.* 6*d.*

—— **Strafford.** Edited by E. H. Hickey. 1*s.* 6*d.*

Burke's Conciliation with America. By Prof. J. Morrison. 1*s.* 6*d.*

Burke's Letters on a Regicide Peace. I. and II. Edited by H. G. Keene, M.A., C.I.E. 1*s.* 6*d.*

Byron's Siege of Corinth. Edited by P. Hordern. 1*s.*

Byron's Childe Harold. Edited by H. G. Keene, M.A., C.I.E. 2*s.* Also Cantos I. and II., sewed, 1*s.* Cantos III. and IV., sewed, 1*s.*

Carlyle's Hero as Man of Letters. Edited by Mark Hunter, M.A. 1*s.* 6*d.*

—— **Hero as Divinity.** By Mark Hunter, M.A. 1*s.* 6*d.*

Chaucer's Minor Poems, Selections from. Edited by J. B. Bilderbeck, M.A. 1*s.* 6*d.*

De Quincey's Revolt of the Tartars and the English Mail-Coach. Edited by Cecil M. Barrow, M.A., and Mark Hunter, M.A. 2*s.*

** Revolt of the Tartars, separately. 1*s.*

—— **Opium Eater.** Edited by Mark Hunter, M.A. 2*s.* 6*d.*

Goldsmith's Good-Natured Man and **She Stoops to Conquer.** Edited by K. Deighton. Each 1*s.*

** The two plays together, 1*s.* 6*d.*

—— **Traveller and Deserted Village.** Edited by the Rev. A. E. Woodward, M.A. Cloth, 1*s.* 6*d.*, or separately, sewed, 10*d.* each.

Irving's Sketch Book. Edited by R. G. Oxenham, M.A. Sewed, 1*s.* 6*d.*

Johnson's Life of Addison. Edited by F. Ryland, M.A. 1*s.*

—— **Life of Swift.** Edited by F. Ryland, M.A. 1*s.*

—— **Life of Pope.** Edited by F. Ryland, M.A. 2*s.*

** The Lives of Swift and Pope, together, sewed, 2*s.* 6*d.*

Johnson's Life of Milton. Edited by F. Ryland, M.A. 1*s.* 1*s.*

—— **Life of Dryden.** Edited by F. Ryland, M.A. 1*s.* 6*d.*

** The Lives of Milton and Dryden, together, sewed, 2*s.* 6*d.*

—— **Lives of Prior and Congreve.** Edited by F. Ryland, M.A. 1*s.*

Kingsley's Heroes. Edited by A. E. Roberts, M.A. Illus. 1*s.* 6*d.* Sewed, 1*s.*

Lamb's Essays. Selected and Edited by K. Deighton. 1*s.* 6*d.*

Longfellow, Selections from, including Evangeline. Edited by M. T. Quinn, M.A. 1*s.* 6*d.*

** Evangeline, separately, sewed, 10*d.*

Macaulay's Lays of Ancient Rome. Edited by P. Hordern. 1*s.* 6*d.*

—— **Essay on Clive.** Edited by Cecil Barrow. 1*s.* 6*d.*

Massinger's A New Way to Pay Old Debts. Edited by K. Deighton. 1*s.* 6*d.*

Milton's Paradise Lost. Books III. and IV. Edited by R. G. Oxenham, M.A. 1*s.* ; or separately, sewed, 10*d.* each.

Milton's Paradise Regained Edited by K. Deighton. 1*s.*

Bell's English - Classics—*continued*

Pope's Essay on Man. Edited by F. RYLAND, M.A. 1s.

Pope, Selections from. Edited by K. DEIGHTON. 1s. 6d.

Scott's Lady of the Lake. Edited by the Rev. A. E. WOODWARD, M.A. 2s. 6d. The Six Cantos separately, sewed, 6d. each.

Shakespeare's Julius Cæsar. Edited by T. DUFF BARNETT, B.A. (Lond.). 1s. 6d.
—— **Merchant of Venice.** Edtied by T. DUFF BARNETT, B.A. (Lond.). 1s 6d.
—— **Tempest.** Edited by T. DUFF BARNETT, B.A. (Lond.). 1s. 6d.

Wordsworth's Excursion. Book I. Edited by M. T. QUINN, M.A. Sewed, 1s.

English Readings

With Introductions and Notes. 16mo.

Burke : Selections. Edited by BLISS PERRY. 2s. 6d.

Byron : Selections. Edited by F. I. CARPENTER. 2s. 6d.

Coleridge : Prose Selections. Edited by HENRY A. BEERS. 2s.

Dryden : Essays on the Drama, Edited by WILLIAM STRUNK. 2s.

Johnson : Prose Selections. Edited by C. G. OSGOOD. 3s.

Milton : Minor English Poems. Edited by MARTIN W. SAMPSON. 2s. 6d.

Swift : Prose Selections. Edited by FREDERICK C. PRESCOTT. 2s. 6d.

Tennyson : The Princess. Edited by L. A. SHERMAN. 2s.

Thackeray : English Humourists. Edited by WILLIAM LYON PHELPS. 2s. 6d.

Readers

The Story of Peter Pan (as told in "The Peter Pan Picture Book."). With 16 Illustrations and Songs from the Play in Tonic Solfa and Old Notation. 9d.

York Readers. A new series of Literary Readers, with Coloured and other Illustrations.
Primer I. 3d. Primer II. 4d.
Infant Reader. 6d.
Introductory Reader. 8d.
Reader, Book I., 9d. Book II., 10d. Book III., 1s. Book IV., 1s. 3d. Book V., 1s. 6d.

York Poetry Books. 3 Books. Paper covers, 6d. each ; cloth, 8d. each.

Poetry for Upper Classes. Selected by E. A. HELPS. 1s. 6d.

Books for Young Readers. Illustrated. 6d. each.
Æsop's Fables.
The Old Boat-House, etc.
Tot and the Cat, etc.
The Cat and the Hen. etc.
The Two Parrots. | The Lost Pigs.
The Story of Three Monkeys.
The Story of a Cat.
Queen Bee and Busy Bee. | Gull's Crag.

Bell's Reading Books. Continuous Narrative Readers. Cloth. Illustrated. 1s. each.
*Great Deeds in English History.
*Adventures of a Donkey.
*Grimm's Tales.
*Great Englishmen. | Great Irishmen.
*Andersen's Tales.
*Life of Columbus.
*Uncle Tom's Cabin.
*Swiss Family Robinson.
*Great Englishwomen.
Great Scotsmen.

Bell's Reading Books—*continued.*
*Gatty's Parables from Nature.
Edgeworth's Tales.
*Scott's Talisman.
*Marryat's Children of the New Forest.
*Dickens' Oliver Twist.
Dickens' Little Nell.
*Masterman Ready.
Marryat's Poor Jack.
Arabian Nights.
Gulliver's Travels.
Lyrical Poetry for Boys and Girls.
Vicar of Wakefield.
*Scott's Ivanhoe.
Lamb's Tales from Shakespeare.
*Robinson Crusoe.
Tales of the Coast.
*Settlers in Canada.
Southey's Life of Nelson.
Sir Roger de Coverley.
*Scott's Woodstock.

* *Cheaper editions of these volumes are issued in limp cloth covers, 6d. net each.*

Bell's Literature Readers. Bound in Cloth. Price 1s. each.
Deeds that Won the Empire. By W. H. FITCHETT, B.A., LL.D.
Fights for the Flag. By W. H. FITCHETT.
Six to Sixteen. By Mrs. EWING.
The Water-Babies. By CHAS. KINGSLEY.
The Last of the Mohicans. By J. FENIMORE COOPER.
Feats on the Fiord. By HARRIET MARTINEAU.
Parables from Nature. By Mrs GATTY.
The Little Duke. By CHARLOTTE YONGE.
The Three Midshipmen. By W. H. G. KINGSTON.

Readers—*continued*

Bell's Geographical Readers. By M. J.
BARRINGTON-WARD, M.A.
The Child's Geography. Illustrated. 6d.
The Round World. (Standard II.) 1s.
About England. (Stand. III.) Illus. 1s. 4d.
Bel 's Animal Life Readers. Designed to
inculcate humane treatment of animals.
Illustrated by HARRISON WEIR and others.
** *Full Prospectus on application.*
The Care of Babies. A Reading Book
for Girls' Schools. Illustrated. Cloth, 1s.
**Bell's History Readers on the Con-
centric Method.** Fully Illustrated.
First Lessons in English History. 10d.
A Junior History of England. 1s. 6d.
A Senior History of England. 2s.

Abbey History Readers. Revised by the
Rt. Rev. F. A. GASQUET, D.D. Illustrated.
Early English History (to 1066). 1s.
Stories from English History (1066-1485).
1s. 3d.
The Tudor Period (1485-1603). 1s. 3d.
The Stuart Period (1603-1714). 1s. 6d.
The Hanoverian Period (1714-1837).
1s. 6d.
Bell's History Readers. Illustrated.
Early English History (to 1066). 1s.
Stories from English History (1066-1485).
1s. 3d.
The Tudor Period (1485-1603). 1s. 3d.
The Stuart Period (1603-1714). 1s. 6d.
The Hanoverian Period (1714-1837). 1s. 6d.

MODERN LANGUAGES
French and German Class Books

Bell's French Course. By R. P. ATHERTON,
M.A. Illustrated. 2 Parts. 1s. 6d. each.
Key to the Exercises, Part I., 6d. net ;
Part II., 1s. net.
Bell's First French Reader. By R. P.
ATHERTON, M.A. Illustrated. 1s.
The Direct Method of Teaching French.
By D. MACKAY, M.A., and F. J. CURTIS, PH. D.
First French Book. 1s. net.
Second French Book. 1s. 6d. net.
Teacher's Handbook. 1s. net.
Subject Wall Picture (Coloured). 7s. 6d.
net.
Bell's French Picture-Cards. Edited by
K. N. ADAIR, M.A. Two Sets of Sixteen
Cards. Printed in Colours, with question-
naire on the back of each. 1s. 3d. net each.
Bell's Illustrated French Readers.
Pott 8vo. Fully Illustrated.
** *Full List on application.*
French Historical Reader. By H. N.
ADAIR, M.A. New Composition Supple-
ment, 2s. ; or without Supplement, 1s. 6d.
Supplement separately, 6d. net.
Contes Français. Anciens et Modernes.
By MARC CEPPI. 1s. 6d. With Question-
naires and Exercises, 2s. Questionnaire,
separately, 6d.
Contes d'Hier et d'Aujourd'hui. First
Series. By J. S. NORMAN, M.A., and
CHARLES ROBERT-DUMAS. Illustrated. 1s. 6d.
Second Series. 2s.
Le Francais de France. By Madame
VALETTE VERNET. With Illustrations. 2s.
Grammaire Pratique. By Madame VAL-
ETTE VERNET. 10d.
Tales from Molière. Edited by MARC
CEPPI, M.A. 1s. 6d. ; or with Vocabulary
and Notes. 2s.
**Stories and Anecdotes for Translation
into French.** By CARL HEATH. 1s.
Essentials of French Grammar. By
H. WILSHIRE, M.A. 1s. 6d.

Gasc's French Course
First French Book. 1s.
Second French Book. 1s. 6d.
Key to First and Second French Books.
1s. 6d. net.
French Fables for Beginners. 1s.
Histoires Amusantes et Instructives. 1s.
Practical Guide to Modern French
Conversation. 1s.
French Poetry for the Young. With
Notes. 1s.
Materials for French Prose Com-
position. 3s. Key, 2s. net.
Prosateurs Contemporains. 2s.
Le Petit Compagnon ; a French Talk-Book
for Little Children. 1s.
By the Rev. A. C. Clapin
French Grammar for Public Schools.
2s. 6d. Key, 3s. 6d. net.
A French Primer. 1s.
Primer of French Philology. 1s.
English Passages for Translation into
French. 2s. 6d. Key, 4s. net.
A German Grammar for Public Schools.
2s. 6d.
A Spanish Primer. 1s.

Bell's First German Course. By L. B. T.
CHAFFEY, M.A. 2s.
Bell's First German Reader. By L. B. T.
CHAFFEY, M.A. Illustrated. 2s.
German Historical Reader. By J. E.
MALLIN, M.A. 2s.
**Buddenbrook : Ein Schultag eines
Realuntersekundaners.** Edited by
J. E. MALLIN, M.A. Illustrated. 2s. 6d.
**Materials for German Prose Com-
position.** By Dr. C. A. BUCHHEIM. 4s. 6d.
A Key to Parts I. and II., 3s. net. Parts
III. and IV., 4s. net.
First Book of German Prose. Being
Parts I. and II. of the above, with
Vocabulary. 1s. 6d.
**Kurzer Leitfaden der Deutschen Dich-
tung.** By A. E. COP. 2s. 6d.

Gasc's French Dictionaries

FRENCH-ENGLISH AND ENGLISH-FRENCH DICTIONARY. Large 8vo. 12s. 6d.
CONCISE FRENCH DICTIONARY. Medium 16mo. 3s. 6d. Or in Two Parts. 2s. each.
POCKET DICTIONARY OF THE FRENCH AND ENGLISH LANGUAGES. 16mo. 2s. 6d.
LITTLE GEM FRENCH DICTIONARY. Narrow 8vo. 1s. net. Limp Leather, 2s. net.

French and German Annotated Editions

Fénelon. Aventures de Télémaque. By C. J. DELILLE. 2s. 6d.

La Fontaine. Select Fables. By F. E. A. GASC. 1s. 6d.

Lamartine. Le Tailleur de Pierres de Saint-Point. By J. BOIELLE, B.-ès-L. 1s. 6d.

Saintine. Picciola. By Dr. DUBUC. 1s. 6d.

Voltaire. Charles XII. By L. DIREY. 1s. 6d.

Gombert's French Drama. Re-edited, with Notes, by F. E. A. GASC. Sewed, 6d. each.

> **Molière.** Le Misanthrope.—L'Avare —Le Bourgeois Gentilhomme.—Le Tartuffe.— Le Malade Imaginaire.—Les Femmes Savantes.—Les Fourberies de Scapin.— Les Précieuses Ridicules.—L'Ecole des Femmes.—L'Ecole des Maris.—Le Médecin Malgré Lui.

Racine. La Thébaïde.—Les Plaideurs.— Iphigénie. — Britannicus. — Phèdre. — Esther.—Athalie.

Corneille. Le Cid.—Horace.—Cinna.— Polyeucte.

Voltaire. Zaire.

German Ballads from Uhland, Goethe, and Schiller. By C. L. BIELEFELD. 1s. 6d.

Goethe. Hermann und Dorothea. By E. BELL, M.A., and E. WÖLFEL. 1s. 6d.

Lessing. Minna von Barnhelm. By Prof. A. B. NICHOLS. 2s. 6d.

Schiller. Wallenstein. By Dr. BUCHHEIM. 5s. Or the Lager and Piccolomini, 2s. 6d. Wallenstein's Tod, 2s. 6d.

—— Maid of Orleans. By Dr. W. WAGNER. 1s. 6d.

—— Maria Stuart. By V. KASTNER. 1s. 6d.

Bell's Modern Translations

A Series of Translations from Modern Languages, with Memoirs, Introductions, etc. Crown 8vo. 1s. each.

Dante. Inferno. Translated by the Rev. H. F. CARY, M.A.

—— Purgatorio. Translated by the Rev. H. F. CARY, M.A.

—— Paradiso. Translated by the Rev. H. F. CARY, M.A.

Goethe. Egmont. Translated by ANNA SWANWICK.

—— Iphigenia in Tauris. Translated by ANNA SWANWICK.

—— Goetz von Berlichingen. Translated by Sir WALTER SCOTT.

—— Hermann and Dorothea. Translated by E. A. BOWRING, C.B.

Hauff. The Caravan. Translated by S. MENDEL.

—— The Inn in the Spessart. Translated by S. MENDEL.

Lessing. Laokoon. Translated by E. C. BEASLEY.

—— Nathan the Wise. Translated by R. DILLON BOYLAN.

Lessing. Minna von Barnhelm. Translated by ERNEST BELL, M.A.

Molière. Translated by C. HERON WALL. 8 vols. The Misanthrope.—The Doctor in Spite of Himself.—Tartuffe.—The Miser.— The Shopkeeper turned Gentleman.—The Affected Ladies.—The Learned Women.— The Impostures of Scapin.

Racine. Translated by R. BRUCE BOSWELL, M.A. 5 vols. Athalie.—Esther.—Iphigenia.—Andromache.—Britannicus.

Schiller. William Tell. Translated by Sir THEODORE MARTIN, K.C.B., LL.D. *New Edition, entirely revised.*

—— The Maid of Orleans. Translated by ANNA SWANWICK.

—— Mary Stuart. Translated by J. MELLISH.

—— Wallenstein's Camp and the Piccolomini. Translated by J. CHURCHILL and S. T. COLERIDGE.

—— The Death of Wallenstein. Translated by S. T. COLERIDGE.

** For other Translations from Modern Languages, see the Catalogue of Bohn's Libraries, which will be forwarded on application.

SCIENCE AND TECHNOLOGY

Detailed Catalogue sent on application

Elementary Botany. By PERCY GROOM, M.A., D.Sc., F.L.S. With 275 Illustrations. 3s. 6d.

Elementary Botany. By G. F. ATKINSON, PH.B. 6s.

Botany for Schools and Colleges. By G. F. ATKINSON. Illustrated. 4s. 6d. net.

Practical Plant Physiology. By FREDERICK KEEBLE, M.A. Crown 8vo. 3s. 6d.

A Laboratory Course in Plant Physiology. By W. F. GANONG, PH.D. 7s. 6d. net.

The Botanist's Pocket-Book. By W. R. HAYWARD. Revised by G. C. DRUCE. 4s. 6d.

An Introduction to the Study of the Comparative Anatomy of Animals. By G. C. BOURNE, M.A., D.Sc. With numerous Illustrations. 2 Vols. Vol. I. Animal Organization. The Protozoa and Cœlenterata. Revised Edition. 6s. Vol. II. The Cœlomata. 4s. 6d.

A Manual of Zoology. By RICHARD HERTWIG. Translated by Prof. J. S. KINGSLEY. Illustrated. 12s. 6d. net.

Injurious and Useful Insects. An Introduction to the Study of Economic Entomology. By Prof. L. C. MIALL, F.R.S. With 100 Illustrations. 3s. 6d.

Civil Service Examination papers: Chemistry Papers, Theoretical and Practical. By A. P. NEWTON. 1s.

A First Year's Course of Chemistry. By JAMES SINCLAIR. 1s.

An Introduction to Chemistry. By D. S. MACNAIR, PH.D., B.SC. 2s.

Elementary Inorganic Chemistry. By Prof. JAMES WALKER, D.SC. 3s. 6d.

Introduction to Inorganic Chemistry. By Dr. ALEXANDER SMITH. 7s. 6d. net.

Laboratory Outline of General Chemistry. By Dr. ALEXANDER SMITH. 2s. 6d.

General Chemistry for Colleges. By Di. ALEXANDER SMITH. 6s. 6d. net.

An Experimental Course in Physical Chemistry. By J. F. SPENCER, D.SC., PH.D. Crown 8vo. 2 vols. 3s. 6d. each.

A Text-book of Organic Chemistry. By WM. A. NOYES. 6s. net.

A Three Years' Course in Practical Physics. By JAMES SINCLAIR. 3 vols. 1s. each.

A College Text-Book of Physics. By A. L. KIMBALL, PH.D. Illustrated. 10s. 6d. net.

The Principles of Physics. By W. F. MAGIE. Illustrated. 7s. 6d. net.

Practical Electricity and Magnetism. First Year's Course. By R. E. STEEL. 2s.

A Text-Book of Gas Manufacture for Students. By JOHN HORNBY. Revised and Enlarged. 7s. 6d. net.

Turbines. By W. H. STUART GARNETT. 8vo. 5s. net.

Electrons. By Sir OLIVER LODGE. 6s. net.

Engines and Boilers. By W. McQUADE. Crown 8vo. Numerous Illus. 3s. 6d. net.

Exercises in Metal Work. By A. T. J. KERSEY, A.R.C.Sc. Crown 8vo. 1s. 6d. net.

Practical Wood Carving for Technical Classes. By F. P. DRURY. 2s. 6d.

Technological Handbooks

Edited by Sir H. TRUEMAN WOOD

Specially adapted for candidates in the examinations of the City and Guilds Institute. Illustrated

Woollen and Worsted Cloth Manufacture. By Prof. ROBERTS BEAUMONT. [*New Edition in preparation.*

Soap Manufacture. By W. LAWRENCE GADD, F.I.C., F.C.S. 5s.

Plumbing: Its Principles and Practice. By S. STEVENS HELLYER. 5s.

Silk-Dyeing and Finishing. By G. H. HURST, F.C.S. 7s. 6d.

Printing. A Practical Treatise. By C. T. JACOBI. 7s. 6d.

Cotton Spinning: Its Development, Principles, and Practice. By R. MARSDEN. 6s. 6d.

Cotton Weaving: Its Development, Principles, and Practice. By R. MARSDEN. 10s. 6d.

Coach Building. By JOHN PHILPSON, M.INST.M.E. 6s.

Bookbinding. By J. W. ZAEHNSDORF. 5s.

The Principles of Wool Combing. By HOWARD PRIESTMAN. 6s.

Music

Music, A Complete Text-Book of. By Prof. H. C. BANISTER. 5s.

Music, A Concise History of. By Rev. H. G. BONAVIA HUNT, MUS. DOC. 3s. 6d.

POLITICAL ECONOMY

Detailed List sent on application

MENTAL AND MORAL SCIENCE

Psychology: A Manual for University Students. By F. RYLAND, M.A. 4s. 6d.

An Introduction to Psychology. By R. M. YERKES. 6s. 6d. net.

Ethics: An Introductory Manual for the use of University Students. By F. RYLAND, M.A. 3s. 6d.

Ethics. By JOHN DEWEY and JAMES H. TUFTS. 8s. 6d. net.

Everyday Ethics. By E. L. CABOT. 5s. net.

Logic. An Introductory Manual for the use of University Students. By F. RYLAND, M.A. 4s. 6d.

The Principles of Logic. By Prof. H. A. AIKINS, PH.D. 6s. 6d.

An Introduction to the Study of Philosophy. By ALICE OLDHAM. 5s. net.

Handbook of the History of Philosophy. By E. BELFORT BAX. 5s.

History of Modern Philosophy. By R. FALCKENBERG. Trans. by Prof. A. C. ARMSTRONG. 16s.

Bacon's Novum Organum and Advancement of Learning. Edited by J. DEVEY, M.A. 5s.

Hegel's Lectures on the Philosophy of History. Translated by J. SIBREE, M.A. Small post 8vo. 5s.

Kant's Critique of Pure Reason. Translated by J. M. D. MEIKLEJOHN. 5s.

Kant's Prolegomena and Metaphysical Foundations of Science. Translated by E. BELFORT BAX. 5s.

Locke's Philosophical Works. Edited by J. A ST. JOHN. 2 vols. 3s. 6d. each.

Modern Philosophers

Edited by Professor E. HERSHEY SNEATH

Descartes. **The Philosophy of Descartes.** Selected and Translated by Prof. H. A. P. TORREY. 6s. net.

Hume. **The Philosophy of Hume.** Selected, with an Introduction, by Prof. HERBERT A. AIKINS. 4s. net.

Locke. **The Philosophy of Locke.** By Prof. JOHN E. RUSSELL. 4s. net.

Reid. **The Philosophy of Reid.** By E. HERSHEY SNEATH, PH.D.

Spinoza. **The Philosophy of Spinoza.** By Prof. G. S. FULLERTON. 6s. net.

HISTORY

Lingard's History of England. Abridged and Continued by DOM H. N. BIRT. With a Preface by ABBOT GASQUET, D.D. With Maps, 5s.; or in 2 vols. Vol. I. (to 1485), 2s. 6d. Vol. II. (1485-1902), 3s.

An Introduction to English Industrial History. By HENRY ALLSOPP, B.A. 2s.

English History Source Books. Edited by S. E. WINBOLT and KENNETH BELL, M.A. 1s. net.

1760-1801: **American Independence and the French Revolution.** [*Now Ready.*

1603-1660: **Puritanism and Liberty.** [*Ready Immediately.*

Full list of series will be sent on application.

First Lessons in English History. Illustrated. 1s.

A Junior History of England. By E. NIXON. Illustrated. 1s. 6d.

A Senior History of England. By A. McKILLIAM, M.A. Crown 8vo. Illus. 2s.

Civil Service Examination Papers: History Questions. By A. PERCIVAL NEWTON, M.A. 1s.

A Practical Synopsis of English History. By ARTHUR BOWES. 1s.

Strickland's Lives of the Queens of England. 6 vols. 5s. each. *** Abridged edition for Schools, 6s. 6d.

Landmarks in the History of Europe. By E. M. RICHARDSON, B.A. Crown 8vo. 2s.

Mediæval Europe, 395-1270. By CHARLES BÉMONT and G. MONOD. Translated under the Editorship of Prof. G. B. ADAMS. 6s. 6d. net.

An Atlas of European History. By EARLE W. DOW. 6s. net.

Duruy's History of the Middle Ages. Translated by E. H. and M. D. WHITNEY. 6s. 6d. net.

The Foundations of Modern Europe. By Dr. EMIL REICH. 5s. net.

Dyer's History of Modern Europe. Revised throughout by ARTHUR HASSALL, M.A. 6 vols. With Maps. 3s. 6d. each.

Life of Napoleon I. By JOHN HOLLAND ROSE, LITT.D. 2 vols. 10s. net.

Carlyle's French Revolution. Edited by J. HOLLAND ROSE, LITT.D. 3 vols. With numerous illustrations. 15s.

Michelet's History of the French Revolution, from its earliest indications to the flight of the King in 1791. 3s. 6d.

Mignet's History of the French Revolution, from 1789 to 1814. 3s. 6d.

Gregorovius' History of the City of Rome in the Middle Ages. Translated by ANNIE HAMILTON. 8 vols. £3. 3s. net. Also sold separately.

Select Historical Documents of the Middle Ages. Translated and edited by ERNEST F. HENDERSON, PH.D. 5s.

Menzel's History of Germany. 3 vols. 3s. 6d. each.

Ranke's History of the Popes. Translated by E. FOSTER. New Edition. Revised. 3 vols. 2s. net each.

Ranke's History of the Latin and Teutonic Nations. Revised Translation by G. R. DENNIS, B.A. With an Introduction by EDWARD ARMSTRONG, M.A. 6s. net.

Catalogue of Historical Books sent post free on application

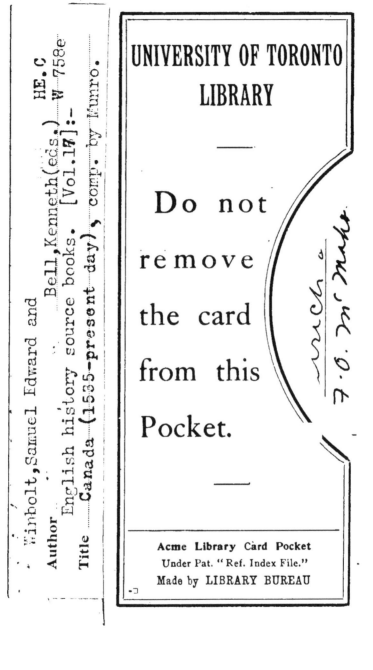

CPSIA information can be obtained
at www.ICGtesting.com
Printed in the USA
BVHW071055040219
539400BV00033B/2348/P